THEY MADE A LIST

a	b		c
<u>a</u>	<u>b</u>		<u>c</u>
apple	birdie	build	clock (tick tock)
all through	bear	flock	comb
auntie	bus		cotton
	book		car
	bye-bye		carriage
	ball		cracker
	baby		cuckoo (cuckoo clock)
	bed		cow (moo-moo)
	bath		h' crying
	brush		cheese
	birdie		cereal
	bells		chair
	banana		clean
	bib		coat
	boat		come
	box		dose (boo)
	bow		cup
	button		
	bridge		
	bandage		
	boy		
	broom		
	back (tick tock)		

THEY
MADE
A
LIST

A MEMOIR BEYOND MEMORY

SUSAN LETZLER COLE

They Made A List: A Memoir Beyond Memory by
Susan Letzler Cole is published by San Diego
State University Press.

No part of this book may be used or reproduced in
any manner whatsoever without prior permission
from San Diego State University Press.

These permissions are waived in the case of
brief quotations embodied in critical
articles and reviews.

San Diego State University Press publications
may be purchased at discount for educational,
business, or sales promotional use.

For information write:

San Diego State University Press
Department of English and Comparative Literature
San Diego State University
San Diego, California, 92182-6020

Cover Design by Isabella Ferrea
Book Design by Guillermo Nericcio García

sdsupress.sdsu.edu

hype.sdsu.edu

amatlcomix.sdsu.edu

Copyright © 2022 Susan Letzler Cole

All rights reserved.

FIRST EDITION

Printed in the United States of America

ISBN: 978-1-938537-19-6

r	s	t
rock, rock	socks soap	train (choo
pow, pow	shoes Susan	thank you
"ring a round a posy"	see-saw Frank	toidy
Ricky	scratch squeeze	there it i
red	sit down street	toast
rag (washdol)	swing sweet	toothbrus
rouge	shade	teeth
read	scrub	tongue
	soldier (tin)	two

v w	y z	
this	yes	tail
that		three
(mama)		toes
		that's a
		tree
		tip toe
—		— trolley
ll		tummy
N		toys

To Kyleelise Holmes Thomas,
who knew what this book was doing
before I did

And Roger Rosenblatt,
whose support for this book was beyond
all measure

ACKNOWLEDGMENTS

The completion of this book would not have been possible without the generous support and assistance of the following people: Jillian Raucci Bedell, Peggy Blumenthal, Marya Bradley, Sara Brzowsky, Alexandra Cannon, Steven Christensen, David Cole, Garrett Dell, Eric Donelson, Alan Edelstein, Pat Flynn, Deborah Frattini, Meg Gertmenian, Elizabeth Gilliam Roberta Michnick Golinkoff, Robert Hubbard, Jeanette Huettner, Amie Keddy, Greg Knobelsdorff, Benjamin Letzler, Kenneth Letzler, Robert Letzler, John Leubsdorf, Kim Mancuso, Jenny Martin, Kelly Matera, Tim Meyers, John McCann, Natalie Miller, Lynn Montez, Madison Neilander, Jerome Nevins, Jefferson Parson, Patti Parson, Jeremy Peterson, Paul Robichaud, Monica D. Rosenberg, Roger Rosenblatt, Christopher Shine, Alexandria Sinchak, Frank Sokolove, Hilda Speicher, Ann Strong, Kyleelise Holmes Thomas, Sarah Wallman.

I deeply appreciate Albertus Magnus College's granting of a sabbatical leave during which I completed a draft of the book, in particular the suppc of the Faculty Welfare and Development Committee.

I am particularly indebted to Dr. William Nericcio, Director of SDSU Press, for his enthusiastic support of this project.

As always, I feel blessed by David Cole's love and by his unwavering beli in this book.

TABLE OF CONTENTS

ntroduction   11

ART 1: NOTICING   14

ART 2: WORDS   87

ART 3: KNOWING AND NOT KNOWING   138

pilogue   180

/orks Cited   182

ILLUSTRATIONS

The List of 200 Words 19
Second Month Entry 34
The Album Cover 116
The Album First Page Inscribed 117
Snapshots:
  "Doll Baby" 4 weeks 119
  "Baby Doll" 120
  "Susan and her old lady" 121
  "What's up?" 5—6 weeks 124
  "Uh Uh, Don't cry!" 124
  "Shhhh!" 125
  "SUMMER SCHOOL": 2 months
    "Pretty Young To Be Reading" 125
    "It's Really Not a Book"
    "It's a Rattle"
"ORANGE JUICE": 7 months
  "Don't Help Me!" 127
  "I Can Hold It Alone!" 127
"A Nice Day in Winter" 8 months 129
"Where *did* they go?" 129
"Where's Daddy?" 8 months 130
"There he is!" 130
"LUNCH TIME": 9 months 132
  "Ma: `Time to eat.'" 132
  "Ma: `See, like this.'" 132
  "Susan: `I like it this way.'" 132
"A Speech" 10 1/2 months 134
The Child's Development and Health Record:
  Title Page 153
  Foreword 154
Alice and Alfred Letzler 165
Parental Notes 168
Snapshots of First Three Months 175

INTRODUCTION

To study language development is to consider the developing mind as it accomplishes one of its most astonishing feats. . .. [T]he questions are likely to outlive the tentative answers.

-Erika Hoff, *Language Development*

The womb is a very noisy place, but it is there that we first hear the voices of those who love us. The sounds of those voices will never be replicated once we take our first breath.

We all know how difficult it is to recover, to "hear" in memory, the voice of a loved one who has died. The question of exactly what sounds we *did* hear in the womb is as unanswerable as the question which most of us think can be answered: what was my first word? This none of us knows with certainty, for it may have been uttered with no listener but oneself, practicing an entrance into the new world of sounds that envelop us as infants.

The Latin derivation of the word *infant* is "[one] unable to speak." How was it that we, alone among mammals, developed the vocal physiology necessary for articulate speech?[1] We are the most helpless of creatures at birth, and yet we, from the start, have the vocal and mental equipment that will eventually allow us to speak any language in the world.

Some years ago, I accidentally found a handwritten list of my 200-word vocabulary at the age of eighteen months. I saw what I expected to see—a mother's hand. To my surprise, I later recognized two hands writing, the hands of my parents, Alice and Alfred Letzler, their comments intermingled: a record of parental acts of noticing a baby's acquisition of language.

I began a search for my first word, my earliest entry into language. The vocabulary of my babyhood was recorded in the form of columns of words (reproduced in chapter 1) positioned beneath each letter of the

---

1. W. Tecumseh Fitch, a cognitive scientist at the University of Vienna, claims that "'A monkey's vocal tract would be perfectly adequate to produce hundreds, thousands of words.'" Carl Zimmer, "Monkeys Could Talk, But Their Brains Aren't Wired for It," *New York Times*, December 13, 2016, D2.

alphabet, an arrangement that does not encourage speculation about chronology.

Seeking likely candidates for my first word among these columned lists, I circle them with questions. I consult contemporary studies of infant acquisition of language. I return with new questions.

I imagine conversations, contexts, interactions in my tiny world of 200 words. I try to gauge when a stream of sounds finally became segmented into "words" and what those words actually meant to me. I invent a strange story I might have told myself, using only my eighteen month-old vocabulary.

I try to imagine a voicelessness I never knew as voicelessness in a world of sounds not my own and what it felt like to have experience (for example, love) without words to express it, as animals must all the time. When I dreamed as a baby, did I dream words never uttered in my non-dreaming life?

I know now that certain sounds simply had to wait until my vocal equipment had developed sufficiently, but I could not have known that then. Learning language as a baby must have been an endless challenge.

In an old-fashioned photo album, captioned snapshots of my babyhood contain words found on my parents' list. In her handwritten captions, my mother creates a child's vocabulary which she is, at the same time, shaping in her daily speech to her baby. Somewhere there must be my first word. Then I discover a small sheet of white unlined paper containing the writing of both parents, my father's comments interposed with my mother's. Their abbreviated phrases and solitary, sometimes illegible words mimic my own earliest attempts at language. The search for my lost first word broadens into, becomes, a recognition of the importance of parental acts of *noticing*, noticing a baby's leap into the world of words and then preserving what otherwise would be lost altogether: the inscription of my words, in words of their own.

Why do I care about this list of my earliest words? Am I looking for what they might tell me about the life that followed my infant language? Am I looking for myself? Am I looking for my parents, long dead, whom I might resurrect by these words? If I could peer into my first words, or the spaces between them, what would I know about my life? Do I learn that we shall never know enough about who we are, and why? During this unimaginable pandemic, upon which I find myself reflecting in some of these pages, we are all perhaps engaged in some such process as is recounted in this book.

The "story" of *They Made a List* is a series of meditations on questions that, in the words of Erika Hoff, "are likely to outlive the temporary answers."[2] These meditations do not form a narrative sequence. They are lenses for different ways of looking. Ultimately, they disclose an initially unvoiced infant and two adults who, amazed by this new being, make lists and keep notes on their firstborn child. Coming upon the language of my infanthood, I discover the voices of those who helped to create and then recorded it.

In this book I write back to the list-makers.

---

[2] Erika Hoff, *Language Development*, 4th ed. (Belmont, CA: Wadsworth, Cengage Learning, 2009), xviii.

PART 1: NOTICING

THEY MADE A LIST

They made a list. I never knew it. Many years after the deaths, I opened and read a large blue book titled *The Child's Development and Health Record,* by Harold O. Ruh and Justin A. Garvin, published in 1928. There m parents had kept meticulous records of weight and height, diet, "development," illnesses, dental events, immunization receipts, accidents, analyses of urine ("for the physician's use"), and favorite presents of their daughter and son from birth to the age of fourteen. The handwriting, in ink and pencil (black, later red, for my brother Kenneth and blue for me), clearly distinguishes my mother's and father's comments. Usually she writes first and my father adds further details. My mother's careful, beautiful handwriting includes exclamation marks and underlining of words for emphasis: "At last! Eating new foods!," "Smart as a whip. . .!" (Kenneth); "<u>Adores</u> movies" (Susan). A droll entry describes her ten-month-old son: "Doesn't take to new foods easily—unless they are on floor."

There are sporadic records of their children's early vocabulary. At eighteen months, the following entry for their daughter appears: "Vocabulary counted up to 200, then stopped taking count."

The list is alphabetized, on two faded sheets of lined white paper, neatly folded in half, written on both sides in pencil. There is no heading. A note on the back of the first page identifies the age and word count of the child who "calls things `mine' and `Susan's.' 1½[years]. Vocabulary—200 words." Susan's words. My words. I count them. I get 197. I count again: 213. The number of words seems to depend on how you treat phrases like "bow wow," "ta ta," "tick tock," and "night night." I decide to accept the count of 200 words.

What world did I inhabit in the presence of listening parents recording my little vocabulary? What if I had only these 200 words? What might happen in this for-a-moment arrested world of language that parents and daughter shared? There is no way to know.

*   *   *

The first word of Charles and Emma Darwin's first child, William Erasmus Darwin, was reported to have been "poor." A few days after her first birthday, their daughter Annie, who died at the age of ten,

"walked unaided for the first time and was heard to say the word `goat.'"
The Darwins were independently wealthy ("millionaires several times
over in today's currency")[3] and there is no record of a favored goat on
the premises. The world these first words unlocked remains
mysterious.[4]

What was my first utterance?

"The triumph of learning a first word is one of the crowning
achievements of human development."[5] Who among us remembers that
moment of crowning achievement?

Was my first word even produced in the presence of a parent?
Perhaps I delivered it privately to myself or to my teddy bear or bunny,
or to a little rocking chair, or to my own toes. Perhaps I might have
begun speaking like the baby daughter Persephone whom Jamaica
Kincaid describes in *See Now Then*: "she walked one step forward before
falling, two steps forward, and balancing herself and staying upright,
and then all across the kitchen floor while at the same time talking not
to herself and not to anyone in particular."[6]

A whole imagined scene rises up and disappears in the unrecorded
life of my first utterance. To recover that lost moment is impossible,
even with 200 words, more or less, with which to try to recreate an

---

3. James D. Loy and Kent M. Loy, *Emma Darwin: A Victorian Life* (Gainesville:
University Press of Florida, 2010), 89, 94, 136.
4. "The possibilities are limitless. This problem is known as the *mapping
problem*. The philosopher Willard Van Orman Quine . . . described the child's
problem as follows: An infinite number of hypotheses about word meaning are
logically possible given the data the child has. Yet children tend to figure out
the meaning of the words that they hear. In fact, children are remarkably able
word learners. From about 18 months, when word learning takes off, until 6
years, children must learn an average of nine new words a day." Hoff, 205.
5. Roberta Michnick Golinkoff and Kathy Hirsh-Pasek, *How Babies Talk: The
Magic and Mystery of Language in the First Three Years of Life* (New York:
Penguin, 2000), 87. Golinkoff and Hirsh-Pasek further note: "Though the
average age of the first word is around 12 months, the normal range is very
wide, starting about 10 months at the low end to 24 months at the high end.
Once vocabulary learning starts, progress is slow and measured. At the end of
this period, most children have amassed about 50 words and vocabulary
learning takes wing. . . . What is it about a first word that is so enthralling? . . .
Is it really so amazing if everyone does it? In many ways, yes . . . ." Golinkoff
and Hirsh-Pasek, 88.
6. Jamaica Kincaid, *See Now Then* (New York: Farrar, Straus and Giroux, 2013),
124.

emergence from sounds and gestures into spoken language, with its tonal differences and shades of meaning.

In his book, *Diary of a Baby*, Daniel Stern says that as a child approaches eighteen months, there is often a

leap into. . .words, . . .symbols and self-reflection. . ..
In some children it starts earlier; in some, later.
The normal range is broad. We don't really know why
 this leap happens exactly when it does. The capacity
 for language and symbolization built into the human gene
 lies dormant until this age. . .. Like the unfolding
 of a flower, a uniquely human one, language blossom
 overnight, when the time is right.[7]

* * *

Here are the words as I found them:

a	*b*	*c*	*d*
apple	birdie	clock (tick tock)	door
all through	bear	comb	daddy
auntie	bus	cotton	dog (bow wow)
	book	car	dress
	bye-bye	carriage	doll
	ball	cracker	duck (kack-kack)
	baby	cuckoo (song book)	Danny (Sragow)
	bed	cow (moo moo)	down
	bath	[s?]he's crying	done
	brush	cheese	dirty
	beads	cereal	he (did)
	bells	chair	dark
	banana	clean	draw
	bib	coat	doctor
	boat	come	ding dong
	box	close (door)	dance
	bow	cup	
	button		
	bridge		
	bandage		
	boy		
	broom		
	back (put back)		
	build		
	block		

---

7. Daniel N. Stern, *Diary of a Baby* (New York: Basic Books, 1990), 119, 111.

e	f	g	h
eye	fruit	grass	here it is
egg	fall down	gloves	hat
		glasses	hair
		grandpa (papa)	hi there
		grandma (gmama)	hand
		good girl	(in the)[crossed out] house
		grape	horse
		green	hop, hop
		goose	hanky

i	k	m	o
	kitty	man	otto
	keys	moon	orange
	kiss	music	orange juice
	knee	more	oh-oh
	king cole	mama	out
	[icon suggesting this was sung]	milk	
		mouth	outside
		mine	
		mouse (Mickey Mouse toy)	
		money	

j	l	n	p
jello	light	nice	piece
	leaf	no	paper
	lap	nose	push
		night night	powder
		no more	page
		noise	please
			(toothpaste) paste
			pipe
			pussy (song)
			penny
			pat
			pocket

q	r	s	t
	rock, rock	socks	train (choo choo)
	"row, row"	shoes	thank you (ta ta)
	[icon suggesting this was sung]	see-saw	
	"ring a round a rosy"	scratch	toidy (ti ti)
	Ricky	sit down	there it is
	red	swing	toast
	rag (washcloth)	shade	toothbrush
	rouge	scrub	teeth
	read	soldier (bear)	tongue
		soap	two
			tail

They Made A List

q	r	s	t
		Susan	three
		spank	toes
		squeeze	that's all
		street	tree
		sweet	tip toe
			trolley
			tummy
			toys

u	v	w	x y z
		what's this	yes
		what's that	
		water (wawa)	
		walk	
ulain [name of maid]		wall	
up		wash	
uncle			

	b	c	d
	birdie build	clock (tick tock)	door
brough	bear block	comb	daddy
tie	bus	cotton	dog (bow wow)
	book	car	dress
	bye-bye	carriage	doll
	ball	cracker	duck (knack-knack)
	baby	cuckoo (tony tick)	Danny (George)
	bed	cow (moo moo)	down
	bath	h'. crying	done
	brush	cheese	dirty
	beads	cereal	he (did)
	bells	chair	dark
	banana	clean	draw
	bib	coat	doctor
	boat	come	ding dong
	box	close (door)	dance
	bow	cup	
	button		
	bridge		
	bandage		
	boy		
	broom		
	back (put back)		

e	f	g	h
eyes	fruit	grace	here it is
egg	fall down	gloves	hat
		glasses	hair
		grandpa (papa)	hi there
		grandma (gmama)	hand
		good girl	~~(mother)~~ house
		grape	horse
		green	hop, hop
		goose	hanky

calls things "mine" and "susan's"

1½ - vocabulary - ~~no words~~ ; puts several words together
them - recognizes a no. of nursery rhymes + songs - calls
bears - makes up games to play with mama, dad
knows place for everything; likes to ~~door~~ alone closet door
~~door~~ and ~~chair~~ just ~~is~~ into place etc - recogn
pictures of mama, daddy + grandpa - imitates
heartily; not completely trained but conscious of every step

k	m	o
kitty	man	otto
keys	moon	orange
kiss	music	orange juice
knee	more	oh-oh
King cole	mama	out
	milk	outside
	mouth	
	mine	
	mouse (mickey mouse toys)	
	money	

l	n	p
light	nice	juice
leaf	no	paper
lap	rose	push
	night night	powder
	no more	page
	noise	please
		paste (toothpaste)
		pipe
		pussy (song)
		penny
		pat
		pocket

q	r	s		t
	rock, pock	socks	soap	train (choo choo)
	"pow, pow"	shoes	Susan	thank you (ta ta)
	"ringa pocket posy"	see-saw	spank	Toidy (ti ti
	Ricky	scratch	squeeze	there it is
	red	sit down	street	toast
	rag (washcloth)	sewing	sweet	toothbrush
	rouge	shade		teeth
	read	scrub		tongue
		soldier (her)		two

u v w	x y z	
whats this	yes	tail
whats that		three
water (wawa)		toes
walk		that's all
rain		tree
up		tip toe
uncle		– trolley
wall		tummy
wash		toys

My world of 200 words was a world without a goat—a world without death or war (despite its being December, 1941). There is a moon (but no sun); there is water (but no rain). There is no illness (there is a scratch and a bandage). There is no recognizable sense of trauma (but there is crying), and no violence (only spanking). There are, wonderfully, books and reading; minor accidents (*fall down*); and many activities: one can *see-saw, swing, walk, tip toe, pat, draw, dance, hop, wash, scrub, scratch, sit down, squeeze, build*, (probably) *sing*.

There are places to be (*house, carriage, bus, boat, car, chairs, lap, outside, street*); food and drink (*apple, banana, cheese, cereal, egg, fruit, grape, jello, toast, orange, orange juice, milk*); persons named and unnamed (*auntie, baby, boy, daddy, Danny, doctor, gmama,* a *good girl, mama, man, papa, Ricky, ulain, uncle,* and *Susan*). There is the inexplicable *otto* (if a person, no one I remember).

There are parts of bodies (*eyes, hair, hand, knee, mouth, nose, teeth, tongue, toes, tummy*). There are animals, of course (*bear, birdie, cuckoo, cow, dog* [*bow wow*], *duck* [*kack kack*], *goose, horse, kitty, mouse, pussy*).

As might be expected, commands are given and received (*close* [the door], *back* [put back], *come, down* [possibly a command], *no more, push, sit down, up* [see comment on "down"]). There are descriptions, explanations, greetings and farewells (*all through, here it is, hi there, bye-bye*); exclamations (*oh-oh*); requests (*please*); questions (*what's this, what's that*); definitive pronouncements (*there it is, that's all*); polite replies (*ta ta* [thank you]).[8]

There are objects to be touched, played with, settled into, worn, wondered at: *ball, beads, bed, bells, bib, block, book, bow, box, broom, brush, button,* clock (*tick tock*), *coat, comb, cotton, cup, doll, door, dress, glasses, gloves, hanky, hat, keys, leaf, money, page, paper, paste* (toothpaste), *penny, pipe, pocket, powder, rag* (washcloth), *rock, rouge, shoes, soap, socks, toothbrush, toys, tree*. There are refusals (*no*) and affirmations (*yes*). There are a few colors, not many: *green*, possibly *orange*, and *red*. There is both light and dark.[9]

---

8. A 2008 "longitudinal study of children's spontaneous speech from 22 to 42 months. . .found that imperatives (i.e., commands) predominate at first, declaratives become the most frequent sentence form by 30 months, and questions are always the least frequent category—but they become more frequent as children get older." Hoff, 238.
9. Listing can be a means of preserving from oblivion what the list contains. A celebrated and poignant example of this would be Sir Nicholas Winton's list—

INTACT IN THEIR MYSTERY

Physics and mathematics professor Brian Greene in his recent book, *Until the End of Time*, provides many explanations for many things, but he tells his readers that "no one knows when we began to speak and why." He adds:

> There is far greater consensus on the early development of the universe. . ... Sound waves, the earliest manifestation of language, rapidly disperse to oblivion. A moment or two after they're produced, they vanish.[10]

That must have been true as well of my earliest language.

There are mysteries folded on mysteries hidden in a simple list of a baby's first 200 words alphabetically arranged. How and why was the vanishing act of my earliest vocabulary preserved from oblivion? In the moments after a word or phrase was uttered, was it written down hurriedly or simply tucked away in memory until someone had a hand (or two) free? Did one parent listen while the other recorded language just emerging from a baby's babble? Did a word need to be repeated several times before it became added to the list? Were certain words never recorded at all?

Toni Morrison, in *The Source of Self-Regard*, mentions a woman named Hannah who may have been a friend of her mother and who seems to be relevant to the writing of her second novel, *Sula*, but she says:

> I don't want to know any more about Miss Hannah Peace, and I'm not going to ask my mother who she really was and what did she do and what were you laughing about and why were you smiling? Because I would like to keep all of my remains and images intact in their mystery. . ...[11]

I do, of course, want to know more and can't ask now what my parents did and were they smiling and laughing. I must be content to allow them and their list to remain intact in a mystery, given and received.

---

left in an attic for half a century—of the 669 children, almost all Jewish, whom he rescued from Czechoslovakia just before the Nazis invaded. His obituary says simply, "He liked lists." *The Economist* (July 11, 2015), 82.

10. Brian Greene, *Until the End of Time: Mind, Matter, and Our Search for Meaning in an Evolving Universe* (New York: Alfred A. Knopf, 2020), 162-163.

11. Toni Morrison, *The Source of Self-Regard: Selected Essays, Speeches, and Meditations* (New York: Alfred A. Knopf, 2019), 241.

LABIODENTALS

About 20,000 or 100,000 years ago, certain sounds simply didn't exist, Joanna Klein tells us. "The transition to eating softer foods changed [adult] bites." Overbites, associated with a softer diet, made labiodentals (sounds made by moving the lower lip against the top teeth, as with the word "fever") easier. "Over thousands of years these sounds could have made their way into language."[12] Apparently, agriculture's effect on language made it somewhat easier to produce sounds like *f* and *v*. This, of course, is a controversial theory, challenging the view that the sounds humans make are related to the development of certain speech organs, cognitive development, changes in the brain.

In my 200-word vocabulary, at the age of eighteen months, there are only two words that begin with f: "fruit" and "fall" (in the phrase "fall down") and no words at all that begin with v. The record of my early speech seems to recapitulate a delay in the production of labiodentals, but it also shows a scarcity of words that begin with e (only two: "eye" and "egg"); j and y (one each: "jello" and "yes"); and i, q, x, and z (none). All this proves nothing, except perhaps that, like labiodentals, there may always be sounds that simply do not seem to exist.

All that noticing can give life to, the list-makers have noticed.

---

12. Joanna Klein, "A Language's Origins in a Few Small Bites," *New York Times*, March 19, 2019, D4.

PROTOPLANETS

During the enforced isolation of the pandemic in 2020-2021, I developed a greater interest in celestial bodies. Scientists have discovered miniature solar flares in the lower layers of the sun's atmosphere. David Berghmans of the Royal Observatory of Belgium says, "We couldn't believe this when we first saw this. And we started giving it crazy names like campfires and dark fibrils and ghosts and whatever we saw."[3]

Our moon seems to have originated after a collision between the earth and a smaller planet. The debris from the impact collected in the moon's orbit around the earth.

What I am most interested in, however, are protoplanets (planets in formation). No one was around to record the early history of the solar system or the formation of the earth. And, as a rule, no one is around to record the early history of a person in formation.

The "protoplanet hypothesis" suggests that the solar system's planets were created after very small objects stuck to each other and then grew bigger. It's not certain precisely what happened next in the process of planet formation.

A "protoperson hypothesis" about language learning might note that small linguistic bits stick to each other and then grow larger and larger. My parents happily were there to record, as accurately as possible, the early history of a person forming language before their eyes then and mine now. The word "planet" derives from the Greek word for "wanderer." In my wandering, what unrecorded "crazy names," like fibrils, did I give to whatever I saw?

---

13. Kenneth Chang, "Up Close and Wearing Heat-Resistant Shades, Probe Spots 'Campfires on the Sun,'" *New York Times*, January 17, 2020, A17.

MOON

For almost three decades after my mother's death, I have continued her nightly ritual of greeting the changing moon. Now I search the moonlit world of my childhood. Perhaps "moon" first appeared in a book read to me.[14] I wonder which of my 200 words had to wait, and for how long, before they met the world beyond books. For Eudora Welty, an encounter with the moon was a defining moment in her life:

> At around six, perhaps, I was standing by myself in our front yard. . .just at that hour. . .when the sun is already below the horizon and the risen full moon in the visible sky. . . begins to take on light. There comes the moment, and I saw it then, when the moon goes from flat to round. For the first time it met my eyes as a globe. The word "moon" came into my mouth. . .. Held in my mouth the moon became a word.[15]

Would I have had such a defining moment in the 200-word world of my infancy? Probably not. But what if I had?

When I was eighteen months old, I accompanied my parents on a visit to Florida. I know this because *The Child's Development and Health Record* reports that I developed an "inflamed throat" with a "high fever of 104," treated by a Dr. Robert Mayer in Miami Beach. I don't remember any of this, though "doctor" is one of my 200 words ("fever" isn't). I find this note: "Auto trip [from Northern Virginia] to Miami Beach, Florida. Took trip well. Acclimated self readily. *Took to ocean without fear*" (italics mine). I wonder if this could have been my "moon" moment. Was that expanse of water I "took to" fearlessly becoming a word in my mouth, a word ("wawa") I was struggling to say?

---

14. Erica Hoff mentions a child who "used the word *moon* to refer to the moon, . . .to hangnails she was pulling off, to half a Cheerio, to curved steer horns mounted on a wall, and to the magnetic capital letter D she was about to put on the refrigerator, to list a few." This feature of young children's language, called "over-extensions," is also illustrated by a child's "calling all adult males *Daddy*." Hoff, 191.
15. Eudora Welty, *One Writer's Beginnings* (Cambridge: Harvard University Press, 1984), 10.

* * *

When did my mother, my father, I myself become a word in my mouth? When my mother became "mama" and my father became "daddy," and I myself by eighteen months became "Susan," what did that mean to me? What *could* it mean?

At what moment did I discover the difference between naming wha was mine alone and what everyone had? There would have been a time when only I was "baby," only I had a "bib," "light" existed only when I was there to see it, "outside" was waiting just for me, and, maybe, just maybe, a risen moon was mine and mine alone.

AN AUTHORIAL SELF

Erika Hoff notes that babies generally learn verbs later than nouns:

> One feature of early vocabularies that has received a great
> deal of attention is the predominance of nouns. . .the
> meanings nouns encode are easier for children to learn than
> are the meanings verbs encode. . ... The easiest words to learn
> through observation are concrete nouns.[16]

In my nonverbal infancy, intimate and collaborative communication
is achieved without words. In my adulthood, words came to dominate
the form of information shared. Who was I in that space between my
infant self, unable to speak, and the evolving, languaged self with which
I came to identify myself and others?

D. P. Wolf suggests that a child begins to develop an "authorial self"
by the age of two. In her view, the child can adopt diverse perspectives
on, or different versions of, the experience of the self.

> Our most immediate definition of self is that of a coherent
> and distinctive center: a bodily container, an anchor point
> for our sense of agency, a single source for our emotions (no
> matter how chaotic), or a kind of volume where the
> chapters of a very personal history accumulate.[17]

In this context, "the authorial self is challenged to incorporate these
different 'versions of the self' into an autobiographical narrative
process" in order "to make sense of the world and of one's own mind
and its various states."[18]

In the earliest stages of the self coming into selfhood through
language, we are each of us a noun becoming a verb.

---

16. Hoff, 188-190. "The noun carries its own weight . . . . It has all it needs. It
contains what Emerson called 'the speaking language of things.'" Roger
Rosenblatt, *Kayak Mourning: Reflections on Love, Grief, and Small Boats* (New
York: HarperCollins, 2012), 70.
17. D. P. Wolf, quoted in Daniel J. Siegel, *The Developing Mind: How
Relationships and the Brain Interact to Shape Who We Are*, 2nd ed. (New York:
The Guilford Press, 2012), 364.
18. Siegel, 365.

PEED WHAT?

A small girl is waiting on a porch as I walk past her house. Ahead of me a woman with a tan, elderly dog approaches. She looks in the direction of the small girl and says, happily: "We can go now, Audrey. He peed."

Audrey: "Peed what?"

"He peed."

"Peed what?"

That little girl could have been me, not yet getting a feel for the difference between transitive and intransitive verbs.

SIGNS

Today on the front porch of Audrey's house are a pair of child's light green boots and a large, empty, silvery dog dish. Several yards to the left of the door is a raised wooden box holding two packed rows of books, protected by a glass window with a handle. A small sign has been placed inside the glass at the front of the box:

This is a "free" library. Take anything
that looks interesting; feel free to return
it if you like. Bring any books that you
would like to add, that you think a neighbor
might like.

Please no textbooks or technical books
[underlined].

Adults on top. Kids below. Enjoy books!
----Lolo

While I am writing down this message, a driver leaves his car and contributes more books.

As I turn the corner, I see another sign attached with thin purple ribbons to the white picket fence at the side of the house. On long white sheets, painted in purple, blue, black and red, are the following words:

Dare [purple] to [black] Dream [blue] of a [black]
World [purple] With [black] No [red] Police [blue]
and [black] No [red] Prisons [purple].

Some of the paint has dripped below the letters, creating a slight Jackson Pollock effect.

A third sign, in a child's shaky handwriting, is pasted to the front door: "In training. Please knock and wait to enter." Whose training? Audrey's? An elderly dog's? Training in what? Peeing more quickly? Writing more carefully? Learning to make polite requests or powerful imperatives?

Only three words in all these signs appear in my first recorded vocabulary: *please, no,* and *book*[s].

Maybe then that was enough.

PANDEMIC

My parents, who lived through the Great Depression and two world wars, would not recognize this new world that has become so familiar. barely can.

People masked, wearing gloves in summer, move apart on streets to create six feet of "social distance" between them and then wave at each other as if the distance has suddenly created an intimacy among strangers. Not the election of Donald Trump in 2016 or the surge of new Congresswomen in 2018 or even the horrid, murderous racism exploding in full view as George Floyd was kneed to death by a policeman in Minneapolis is as unimaginable as the coronavirus that began sweeping around the world in 2020.

Schools, stores, sports, restaurants, bars, beaches, doctors' and dentists' offices, public parks and campgrounds, even the Eiffel Tower have been removed for months from public access. Refrigerated tracto: trailers hold an overflow of dead bodies in New York. Saudi Arabia drastically cuts back the hajj for perhaps the first time in history; the traditional pebbles pilgrims throw at the devil are sterilized. Berlin an New York cancel their marathons and ball players are prohibited from spitting. The Supreme Court hears its cases by telephone.

After a cold May where, for about ten minutes, it snowed in New Haven, June—the month of my birth, my wedding anniversary, Dad's death—is suddenly blistering in its heat. A lone boy shoots baskets in an abandoned school yard. An African-American woman in the passenger seat of a passing car rolls down the window and says sweetly "I like your yellow hat," as I stand at an intersection. A perfectly-forme bird nest sits atop a parked car. A black dog walking with his family of three turns his gaze steadily on me as I pass by. A young man walking rapidly down the sidewalk ahead of me holds a small radio announcing fear for Reverend Al Sharpton's safety as he travels around the country

My daily walks grow longer and longer. I smile at strangers whose eyes crinkle above their face masks, their voices muffled. I look, I liste I navigate the world without speaking. In the midst of so much loss, I have found my way back to my earliest preverbal self, the languageless being my parents knew so well so long ago.

TALKING

A note in my mother's hand on page 15 of her copy of *The Child's Development and Health Record* says, "Turns to light. Smiles and `talks' in response. . .. Entertains self by `talking,' holding head erect and looking around, clawing and sucking [cloth] diaper under head." I am two months old, lying on my stomach. I turn to the light. Head erect, eyes alert, hands clawing, mouth sucking, I am "talking": to the woman recording her child's development, to myself, to the light.

An earlier entry (under "Birth to One Month") mentions that the child "[s]tarts at loud sounds. Closes eyes in bright light." Did I "start" at my own loud sounds? Did I always know they were mine?

Sometime between one month and two months, I stop closing my eyes to the light and turn toward it. Sometime between one month and two months, I begin to "talk." Did my "talking" sound like a sound that would never startle me? When did it aim itself at other sounds?

Only now do I begin to wonder if the talk of my babyhood, performed in response to the melodic voice of my mother, gave staying power for the future soundscapes of my life as teacher and writer.

I must often have talked to myself when no one was around to record my sounds, scavenging my tiny word-hoard, maybe telling stories lost forever. Something like this: *A small girl arrives. She is without fear. In her suitcase she carries 200 words with which she intends to soothe any pain, answer to every desire, evoke the unimaginable life of her future self.*

Many things happen to this girl. A bear claims to be her aunt; a birdie puts buttons on her box of beads. A clock is crying somewhere; a book bells her (she has no word for "home"). In a house of jello, a hat dances. A horse hops toward her hanky; on the grass beside papa and gmama, a goose wearing gloves and glasses eats a green grape. A dark door in a dirty dress greets her. A hanky eyes an egg: fruit falls down; Kitty's keys kiss the knee of King Cole.

What's this? What's that?

There it is!

That's all.

SECOND MONTH

PHYSICAL EXAMINATION:

Nutrition: *excellent* Skin: *clear*
Eyes: *occasion[al] tearing* Ears: *negative* Nose: *negative*
Mouth: *negative* Throat: *normal*
Thymus: *negative* Thyroid: *normal* Neck glands: *no enlarged*
Lungs: *clear*
Heart: *normal*
Abdomen: *normal*
Hernia: *corrected* Genitalia: *negative*

Habits: *normal*

T.   P.   R.

DEVELOPMENT: While lying on stomach, holds head & chest up, raise[s]
legs, supports self only on stomach. Holds head erect, while held
over shoulder, for long periods at time. Turns to light.
Smiles and "talks" in response. Likes oil & orange juice from
start. Loves bath but dislikes cool water sponging. Entertains self
"talking", holding head erect and looking around, clawing and sucking
finger, under head. Before 2 mos. old turned over in crib from
front to back. Given rattle, holds it & coos at it.

DIET: Formula — 12 oz milk, 18 oz water, 3 tb. Dextri-maltose #1
6th week { 12 oz milk, 8 oz water, 3 tb Dextri-maltose
           oleum percomorphum
           orange juice

Kenneth Development

~~HABITS~~: Much like Susan, but turned from front to ba[ck]
first in 3rd month. Enjoys having Susan "cha[t]"
with him. Very friendly.

Diet — Started Pablum at 6 weeks — work up to 4-6 tea[sp.]
at 6 PM + 10 AM feedings

[15]

STORIES

Why do we tell stories to, and for, and as, children? I, like most children, was interested in hearing, then pretending to read (after memorizing), all sorts of stories. As an adolescent, I entertained spellbound younger New York cousins after Thanksgiving dinner with my half-remembered, half-created tales, told in a darkened back bedroom of Grandpa and Grandma's Upper West Side apartment at 468 Riverside Drive.

So much happens so effortlessly, only to be retrieved by effort.

Lucretius writes: "The child, like a sailor cast forth by the cruel waves, lies naked upon the ground, speechless, in need of every kind of vital support, as soon as nature has spilt him forth with throes from his mother's womb into the regions of light."[9] Speechless, in the dark, then spilled forth into the regions of sound and (bright) light, we open our mouths and eyes in astonishment. Our story-telling recreates that primal world where what we see and hear and finally "speak" is ours and ours alone, created *ex nihilo* as we spill forth from the womb. Starting at loud sounds, closing my eyes in bright light, the child I was makes her way to the pleasures of language and illumination. At some point "made-up" stories and "facts" must have become distinct, but when, and how, exactly?

As a young child, I would not answer my mother's call until she uttered the name I had chosen for myself that day—Little Red Riding Hood, Gretel, some heroine in a book I loved.

I wasn't telling stories: I was becoming them.

---

19. Lucretius, "On the Nature of Things," quoted by Stephen Greenblatt, "The Answer Man," *The New Yorker*, August 8, 2011, 51.

UTERUS

Three years ago I saw my uterus. Not so unusual. Pregnant women do this all the time. But I am not, and never have been, pregnant.

After a transvaginal ultra sound, a young technician asks if I want to look at the pictures she has been taking, points at the screen, and says, "That's your uterus." How remarkable: such a small territory, almost unnoticed in a greyish space resembling images I had seen of the uninhabited landscape of Mars, is in fact the place where so much life is generated.

This hollow muscular organ in the pelvic cavity of the female mammal is the first home we leave and like our infanthood, only images of it remain.

And I sit here using words to search their origins in my own life.

THIS WOULD BE IMPOSSIBLE

It has been claimed that, unlike chimpanzees and other primates, humans are born prematurely. Indeed, as Michael Corballis suggests, "to conform to the general primate pattern, human babies should be born at around eighteen months, not nine months, but as any mother will agree, this would be impossible, given the size of the birth canal."
Our prolonged childhood means that the human
brain undergoes most of its growth while exposed
to external influences and is therefore more
finely tuned to its environment. Moreover, this
allows the brain to grow larger relative to body
size than it does in any other primates.[20]
I would not want to lose the advantage of a larger brain, but what if humans were born at around eighteen months?

Think about it. There would be a decrease in a baby's ever-inventive gestural "language" and babbling that precede spoken language. Since vocal equipment would be more advanced, two- or three-word phrases would quickly emerge. There would almost certainly be no interest in the discovery of a first word.

In the flurry of word-sounds present in this new world, "words" would fly out ahead of any clear understanding of their sense or reference. There would be no early private language. Talking to myself would lose its necessity, perhaps disappear, as I quickly became a public speaker among other public speakers, using a common, shared language. My increasingly recognizable vocabulary would burgeon, displacing the self-created lexicon of baby sounds. There might be loss of an inner life, less experimenting and need for rehearsal in producing word chains, probably fewer quizzical looks and questionings of what I meant (perhaps leading to fewer parent-child verbal interactions).

I would quite soon join the conventional, "normal" speech of those around me. There would be no "my words," just everybody's. Much of my proto-language would be entirely lost, never recovered. Certain cries, songs, odd syntax would not be on display. I would simply lose the creative infanthood that separated me from a too-early entry into a very different world.

I would lose the most private speaking self I ever had.

---

20. Michael C. Corballis, *From Hand to Mouth: The Origins of Language* (Princeton: Princeton University Press, 2002), 90.

THE STORY THAT BECAME ME

"Now psychologists tell us that babies are intellectually rich and hypothesis-forming and goal-directed," Adam Gopnik writes in *The New Yorker*. He adds: "We, creatures of language who organize our experiences in abstract concepts, can't imagine what it's like to be in the head of a being that has no language." He is talking here about dogs who "speak our language without actually speaking any, and share our concerns without really being able to understand them."[21]

We in our intellectually rich but language-poor babyhood tell ourselves stories that hypothesize what we do not yet understand. When does "really being able to understand" become one of our goal-directed activities? At two months old, I am said to be entertaining myself by "talking" as I look about. Am I trying to make sense of my surroundings; speaking my own language; reorganizing, "fictionalizing" my experience? Is this the origin of story-telling?

The "story" I am trying to tell here can only be imagined. How can I know what it was really like to be *me* at the age of two months, or eighteen months, even with the help of devoted, note-taking parents' records of their child's behavior and vocalizations. The philosopher Thomas Nagel, writing about bats, says:

> It will not help to try to imagine that. . . one has very poor vision, and perceives the surrounding world by a system of reflected high-frequency sound signals. . . . In so far as I can imagine this (which is not very far), it tells me only what it would be like for *me* to behave as a bat behaves. I want to know what it is like for a *bat* to be a bat. Yet if I try to imagine this, I am restricted to the resources of my own mind, and those resources are inadequate to the task.[22]

21. Adam Gopnick, "Dog Story: How did the dog become our master?," *The New Yorker*, August 8, 2011, 51, 52.
22. Thomas Nagel, "What Does It Feel Like to Be a Bat?," quoted by Gopnik, "Dog Story," 52. Kathryn Schulz writes: "All my memories can't add up to a single moment of what it was like to be my father." Kathryn Schulz, "Losing Streak: Reflections on two seasons of loss," *The New Yorker*, February 13 & 20, 2017, 75.

A baby can imitate particular behaviors (smiling, repeating sounds, looking at eyes looking at mine) without knowing what it is like to be the person she imitates. To know myself as an infant is to know as I once did, by resources "inadequate to the task."

* * *

Fiction, an "imaginative creation or a pretense that does not represent actuality but has been invented," has as its Latin root *fictio, fiction < fictus,* p. part. of *fingere,* to form.[23] What did I form after I "spilt. . .forth. . .into the regions of light"? With my 200 words, I could call out to, summon, question, sing to, affirm, negate, greet much of what lay in my path or entered my small world. Perhaps I had formed a language of my own, lost and replaced by words my parents taught me. After I emerged into a region of bright light and strange new sounds, perhaps "actuality" seemed an invented world, a pretend world that invited me to join its pretense since there was no going back to the womb-world I had known. How remarkable it seems that any of us achieves that transfer. If as infants we don't understand the new realm we have entered, we do, nonetheless, accommodate ourselves to its bizarre differences.

So who or what was the story that became me? What did I know without knowing very much? Who, in fact, was I while loving parents carefully recorded my words?

I lived among concrete things whose shape or color or function or taste or kinetic and tactile nature drew my attention. I was a "Susan," not an "I." (But what exactly was a name to me, then?) I didn't seem to know my parents' names, and yet I knew a little boy my age called Danny—and a Ricky (and perhaps the mysterious Otto). Three or so names in my word-hoard, but what did they name? Certainly they were sounds that distinguished one entity from others. Was there only one Susan in the world? Was something "mine" because I wanted it or because no one else could have this particular "tummy" or "tongue" or "nose"? What did I understand of the relationships I inadvertently identified when I called my parents "mama" and "daddy"?

How much of the womb-world did I remember? Did I know that I had once lived inside my mama, not my daddy? Did I know that there

---

23. *The American Heritage Dictionary,* 4th ed. (Boston: Houghton Mifflin, 2002), 515.

could be other mamas in the world, but only one had shared her body with me? These are questions that outlive tentative answers.

So I come full circle. The reality of my womb-home is already a stor I must imagine, before I can meet my own beginnings. What I as an infant had to "form" going forward, I as an adult have to "form" going back, as far back as my first home, an elsewhere. Like the philosopher Thomas Nagel, "in so far as I can imagine this (which is not very far), . . I am restricted to the resources of my own mind, and those resources are inadequate to the task."

How ironic that in wishing to re-enter the 200-word world of my babyhood, I am baffled by this earlier world of my own wordlessness, a womb-world of sounds not my own.

SOUND

I imagine the otherness of my earliest life. I am in the dark, literally and metaphorically. I cannot see or speak in my fluid-filled amniotic sac, but I hear your voices. I feel movement, the movement of what surrounds me, the movement of the woman who carries me within her. "Took trip well. Acclimated self readily. Took to ocean without fear." The womb is our first ocean, our original acclimated self, our first acclimatization of self to "world."

If, in that pre-birth enclosed ocean, I could have imagined a future life for myself, what would it be like? A world of sound but no "language"; a world of movement but no discernible goal; a world wet, dark, close at hand; a world in which every sensation is just that. There would be no boredom for there would be no experience of what else was possible; there would be no speculation for there would be only the present; there would be no unsatisfied curiosity for all experience would have been, well, experienced. There might be pain or discomfort but this would be just another sensation. There would be no fear of death, no search for "truth" beyond existence, no foreboding, time-pressures, work load, deadlines, laundry, email, suicide bombers, rent to pay, food to purchase, clothes to covet, people to meet. There would be no sex, no love, no pandemics. . .. So many exclusions, but what if this first fluid world were exactly that—fluid?

Maybe the sounds of my parents' voices embed themselves in my membranous labyrinth, those fluid-filled sacs of my inner ears, and I begin to shape my movements in response to rhythmic patterns. Maybe I am dancing in the dark. Maybe sound is my first hint of a world elsewhere.[24] Maybe sound is simply what my world is made of. I am nourished invisibly by the placenta which partially envelops me. I grow. I move. The umbilical cord is my lifeline and though I do not know this, it will be cut, and for the first time I will use my own lungs to breathe, to make the human sounds I have already heard but never uttered. Voicing will be my lifeline then.

---

24. In *The Universal Sense: How Hearing Shapes the Mind*, Seth Horowitz writes, "Hearing is our exploratory sense, the one that reaches out ahead and behind us, in dark and light." He notes that "hearing is an objectively faster processing system [than vision]. While vision maxes out at fifteen to twenty-five events per second, hearing is based on events that occur thousands of times per second." Seth S. Horowitz, *The Universal Sense* (New York: Bloomsbury, 2012), 260, 98.

I find my earliest self in sound—the voices I hear before I am born and the voice I give birth to at my birth. In search of that "self," that "Susan," I must give voice to what I once knew: my own voicelessness, re-enter it to find voice.

I try to imagine a voicelessness I never knew *as* voicelessness. Without being able to speak, I must have had no sense of voice as anything *but* elsewhere. Voice would be my earliest relation to what was other and yet near. How could I know what it was I first heard? It would be a sound from outside my world, a sound I would never again hear in that way.

TIME

In the womb, time must have no meaning. I try to imagine that now.

It is not an adult sense of present-ness, not a "living in the moment." It would be a life without moments—a fluidity of being in which I develop, enlarge, take on form involuntarily. The breath of life—oxygen—flows toward me, blood red, through an umbilical cord. "Pictures" can be taken of me at various stages, movements can be felt, private organs detected. I eavesdrop without embarrassment or violation as I accompany another being in her every waking and sleeping moment. I can travel, go to an office or a play, be present while my mother urinates, defecates, vomits—or makes love. I am, in a literal sense, more intimately connected to another living person than I can ever be again and yet intimately connected to someone I have not met.

And all this while time has no meaning.

AN ORCHESTRA

Oliver Sacks has described the human brain as "a vastly complicated orchestra with thousands of instruments, an orchestra that conducts itself, with an ever-increasing score and repertoire." He adds that he finds himself "uncertain whether words, symbols, and images of various types are the primary tools of thought or whether there are forms of thought antecedent to all of these, forms of thought essentially amodal."[25] My search for my first word is a search for the first instrument in the orchestra of my mind.

Did my first intelligible sound "conduct" others in what would be "an ever-increasing score and repertoire"?

It is fascinating to imagine my infant word-hoard as interacting instruments, the music of the mind coming into language from forms antecedent to all the tools of thought I rely on now.

* * *

Long ago, I played the clarinet in my high school orchestra. On one occasion, the student playing the triangle was absent and for some reason I was asked to take his place. (Perhaps my contribution as a clarinetist was not indispensable.) Standing in the back of the rehearsal room, far from the music director, I found myself not looking at the score but listening to the sounds of multiple instruments that suddenly seemed to be conducting themselves. I was simultaneously rapt and paralyzed by a sense of unfamiliarity. The piece ended without my ever striking the triangle.

Our teacher asked us to play the same piece again. This time the triangle trill was heard, adding what Walter Piston calls its "high, clear and luminous"[26] tone of indefinite pitch to the other sounds of the orchestra. I barely remember how I accomplished this, but I remember the teacher, never criticizing or embarrassing me, pointing out to the

---

25. Oliver Sacks, *The Mind's Eye* (New York: Random House, 2010), 104, 226. Seth Horowitz describes the brain as "a neuronal orchestra." *The Universal Sense*, 227.

26. Walter Piston, *Orchestration* (New York: Norton, 1955), 313. Piston adds, "The triangle is of such outstanding effect that it must be used with extreme economy. The trill is especially liable to abuse, and. . .possesses an unfortunate resemblance to certain electric bells, the telephone bell in particular." This I am glad I did not know.

other students that it was important that Susan was listening first before adding to the sounds of the orchestra.

In the evolving brain of the baby, the "orchestra that conducts itself" is created by listening and later performing for others, without criticism or embarrassment, even without prior experience of each new instrument or its effects.

Michio Kaku has observed that "the two greatest mysteries in all of nature are the mind and the universe." He adds, "There are 100 billion stars in the Milky Way galaxy, roughly the same as the number of neurons in our brain. You may have to travel twenty-four trillion miles, to the first star outside our solar system, to find an object as complex as what is sitting on your shoulders."[27]

What was sitting on my shoulders as a baby was an orchestra playing in a galaxy so close and so far away.

---

27. Michio Kaku, *The Future of the Mind* (New York: Random House, 2014), 1-2.

TALKING WITH THEIR HANDS

A headline in the Sports section of the *New York Times* reads: "In a High-Tech Era, Ball Clubs Still Talk With Their Hands." Apparently, signs in baseball originated during the Civil War, "inspired by signals used in battle."[28] Talking with our hands goes back a lot further, and had multiple sources of "inspiration" in the lives of our primate ancestors.

Michael Corballis argues that "human language evolved first as a system of manual gestures," similar to the communication system of chimpanzees and bonobos 5 million years ago.[29] We are born with a vocalization, however inarticulate, but "in human ontogeny, gestures are a stepping stone to the first words."[30] We point, we babble, and then, finally, we arrive at one- or two-word vocal communication.

"You don't appreciate how much you need to see your hands until you can't," Farhad Manjoo reminds us. "Your hands—they're always there. Even in the most immersive of media experiences."[31] Brain scan on children suggest that handwriting can change brain function and development.[32]

---

28. Wayne Epps, Jr., "In a High-Tech Era, Ball Clubs Still Talk With Their Hands," *New York Times*, July 14, 2016, B9.

29. Corballis, 32. He adds: "The chimpanzee, along with the bonobo, is our closest relative among the great apes. This makes it likely that the common ancestors of ourselves and these two species, dating from about 5 million year ago, would have been much better equipped to develop a communication system based on manual and bodily gestures than one based on vocalization." Ibid.

30. James R. Hurford, *The Origins of Grammar: Language in the Light of Evolution* (Oxford: Oxford University Press, 2012), 120. Ernst Haeckel's famous theory that ontogeny recapitulates phylogeny has been questioned but still retains some influence. Hurford notes: "A plausible way-stage in the transition from ape communication was a gestural protolanguage, which gradually gave way to a spoken protolanguage. The gestural origins of language have been advocated extensively, and there is a growing appreciation of the plausibility of the idea." Ibid., 115.

31. Farhad Manjoo, "Virtual Reality's Unsettling Rabbit Hole," *New York Times* June 23, 2016, B1.

32. Karin James, a professor at Indiana University who has done brain scans on children, says: "My overarching research focuses on how learning and interacting with the world with our hands has a really significant effect on our cognition, . . .on how writing by hand changes brain function and can change

Watching reruns of *Cagney and Lacey*, a television series about two female police detectives, I see Mary Beth Lacey, played by Tyne Daly, holding her new baby, Alice, named after her mother, as she talks intimately with her teenage son. We hear unintelligible cooing, then more insistent babbling. Mary Beth adjusts the position of the child cradled in her arms and continues her conversation with her son. The baby reaches upward, partly eclipsing the actress' face, her tiny fingers touching and exploring her lips. Tyne Daly, an extraordinarily accomplished actress, continues Mary Beth's dialogue with her older child after pausing, in a seemingly spontaneous gesture, to kiss the tiny hands of her baby.

Later I replay that scene in my mind. The baby was talking with her hands. She momentarily diverted the conversation above her head. Perhaps she was trying to stop or join the talking that excluded her. Perhaps she was trying to explore the unseen (and as yet undeveloped in her own body) "articulators" of the vocal tract[33] that produce sounds she could not yet make. The mother's lips kissed the baby's hands, precursors to the production of language.

Alice was my mother's name. I imagine her as baby, trying to join a conversation between her mother and her older brother. Alice would be gesturing, babbling, finally touching the seeming source of sounds she could not replicate. In this imagining of a scene I never could have seen, I begin to visualize her entry into talking with her hands.

In giving her baby the name of her own mother, Mary Beth Lacey is, in a sense, rebirthing the woman who gave birth to her. I reverse that here, imagining in the babyhood of my mother the gestural origins of speech in her own daughter.

---

brain development." Perri Klass, "Writing to Learn," *New York Times*, July 21, 2016, D6.

33. Corballis identifies "six independent `articulators' in the vocal tract. These are the lips, the blade of the tongue, the body of the tongue, the root of the tongue, the velum (or soft palate), and the larynx (or `voice box')." With the exception of the movements of the lips, we mainly do not see what Corballis calls "the various distortions of the vocal tract that allow us to produce the different sounds of speech [which] can be regarded as *gestures*. . .when we watch people speaking." *From Hand to Mouth*, 140-141.

SMART ENOUGH

In his wonderfully titled book, *Are We Smart Enough to Know How Smart Animals Are?*, primatologist and ethologist Frans de Waal says, "No one serious about language evolution will ever be able to get around animal comparisons."[34] It has been reported that an Asian elephant named Koshik, putting his trunk inside his mouth, uses it "to modulate the tone and pitch of sounds his voice makes" with such precision that he can emulate the speech of his keepers. His small vocabulary includes the Korean words for *hello, sit down, lie down, good,* and *no.* Researchers say that Koshik "started to imitate his keepers' sounds only after he was separated from other elephants at the age of 5—and that his desire to speak like a human arose from sheer loneliness."[35]

The honeyguide, through a series of excited twitters, can show the Yao people of northern Mozambique the location of beehives. Natalie Angier writes that this bird can be "recruit[ed]. . . with a distinctive vocalization, a firmly trilled `brr' followed by a grunted `hmmm'. . .. How this alliance [between humans foraging for honey and honeyguides rewarded with leftover beeswax] began remains mysterious, but it is thought to be quite ancient." It has been suggested that the bird "might even have played a role in the emergence of fully modern humans and their energetically demanding brains."[36]

I know that human babies in utero can distinguish their mother's voice from that of others, but startling to me is the news that some female birds can teach their babies to sing before they are born. After female Australian superb fairy wrens repeat one vocalization again and again when incubating their eggs, the baby birds, once hatched, make an identical chirp. This finding "hints that effective embryonic learning

---

34. Frans de Waal, *Are We Smart Enough to Know How Smart Animals Are?* (New York: Norton, 2016), 109.
35. Russell Goldman, "Korean Words, From an Elephant," *New York Times*, May 27, 2016, A6.
36. Natalie Angier, "African Tribesmen Can Talk Birds Into Helping Them Find Honey," *New York Times*, July 24, 2016, 6N. Angier notes that "honey is among the most energy-rich foods in nature." Equally fascinating is the famous "honeybee dance-language communication," a waggle dance that "convey[s] information to nestmates about the location of rich food sources." May Berenbaum, "Understanding Apis," *Times Literary Supplement* (July 8, 2016), 22–24.

could signal neurological prowess of progeny to parents."[37] The young birds that most closely imitate their mother's voice are given the most food.

Frans de Waal mentions the "FoxP2 gene that affects both human articulated speech and the fine motor control of birdsong. Science increasingly views human speech and birdsong as products of convergent evolution, given that songbirds and humans share at least fifty genes specifically related to vocal learning."[38] In my search for the origins of my own "language evolution," there is no way I can get around animal comparisons.

---

37. Rachel Nuwer, "Eggshell Education," *Scientific American*, vol. 314, no. 6 (June 2016), 20.
38. de Waal, 109.

ALIENS

During a spirited discussion on NPR of what we could send to an alien planet that might represent life on earth, one participant suggests birdsong, explaining her choice on the basis of the sheer pleasure of the sounds.

Like human infants, "young songbirds have a babbling phase and learn their songs by listening to and imitating adult tutors," Virginia Morrell remarks in *Animal Wise*. "They also dream about new songs they're learning, replaying them. . ., something scientists discovered by comparing the brain activities of zebra finches as they sang during the day and slept at night."[39] Apparently the human ear cannot hear the full repertoire of the birds visible to the eye; only if we were a bird could we know what it is that we are actually listening to. Would alien beings, if they could communicate with us, if they could send us *their* birdsongs, have heard all the sounds the birds themselves offered or responded to? Would they actually hear more of the sounds of our earth than we do? If we contacted an alien world and learned how its inhabitants listen, would sound itself become a new phenomenon?

And if all this were to happen in the far-away future, our first utterance might be the sound of birdsong.

---

39. Virginia Morrell, *Animal Wise: The Thoughts and Emotions of Our Fellow Creatures* (New York: Crown, 2013), 89.

5:30 A.M.

There is a mainly dead tree outside our bedroom window with clumps of brownish leaves, a frequent resting place for the small, ubiquitous, brownish birds who torment me with their calls to each other in the early hours of the morning. This morning, awakened by insistent chirping, I knock on the glass pane of the window. The sounds cease. There is a flurry of wings and a flight headed directly to the tree nearby. The bird and I seem to catch each other's eye and we hold that stance for several minutes. After I leave my post at the window, the loud chirping begins again. Now I listen more closely to the language I am hearing. There is a steady staccato, then a pause, then a new single sound, then a kind of trill. Of course my mother would have known what these birds were, by their appearance and song, but I imagine myself as her baby, born in early June, hearing birds in the morning, their wordless language anticipating my own, giving me a model of cries that would announce my presence and present needs.

What was I learning then from sounds not my own?

THE BRAIN-MACHINE

I learn that speaking requires "the precise control of almost 100 muscles in the lips, jaw, tongue and throat to produce the characteristic breaths and sounds that make up sentences."[40] Well, I knew it was hard, but not that hard. Now it almost seems easier to be typing these words than to utter them aloud. It's probably the word "precise" that impresses me most. I usually think of precision as I try to find the right words or phrases, after which saying them seems so simple.

There is a new field, brain-machine interface technology, that produces synthesized speech from brain signals without requiring muscle movement. At least 70 percent of the simulated speech is intelligible. The new program "generates about 150 [words] a minute, the pace of natural speech."[41] When exactly did 70 percent of what I spoke become intelligible and were there unrecorded guesses about the other 30 percent? Maybe 150 words a minute was the pace of my baby babble, "words" unintelligible to listeners other than myself. Certainly it could have been the pace of the insistent bird chatter in the trees on the front lawn every spring.

Maybe in our early life we are chirping our way into language.

---

40. "A Real Brain Wave: How to Give Voice to the Speechless," *The Economist*, vol. 430, no. 9140 (April 27, 2019), 70.
41. Benedict Carey, "Hope for the Voiceless: Scientists Decode Brain's Vocal Signals," *New York Times*, April 25, 2019, B4.

THE MOURNING DOVE

Walking a few feet ahead of me on the sidewalk is a silent mourning dove. Its head bobbles rapidly in a disconcerting way as it pecks at various microscopic remnants of a late afternoon downpour. Its feet, usually described as bright reddish-pink, appear orange today, quite a dapper look.

Each day, early and late, I hear the mournful sounds of the doves that live somewhere behind our apartment building: ooah, cooo, cooo, coo. My "oh-oh" could conceivably have been my closest approximation to the mourning dove's "ooah," but more likely it was a mimicking of my parents' reaction to some mess I made.

We are told that songbirds and humans share many genes related to vocal learning. There is no record of my attempt to imitate the cries of any of the birds that would have been audible every spring and summer in Virginia.

Apparently, I didn't get the memo.

A LITTLE CHINESE GIRL

Three generations of a family from China—grandparents, parents, and their daughter—live in a nearby apartment. A small outdoor passageway between their building and ours connects the front courtyard and the parking lot in the back. Residents entering from one side and those entering from the other side often meet midway on this narrow path.

As I walk into the passageway, I see a little Chinese girl walking toward me. Her parents carefully reposition her on the nearby grass. She watches me as I continue to walk and wave to her with my right hand. She raises her right hand in imitation of mine. Then her hand stops in front of her chest, palm outstretched, in a silent gesture that seems both formal and foreign, as if she were addressing me in her own language.

The girl knows no English. I know no Chinese. We have communicated in our own gestural language, perfectly understood.

I try to imagine the gestures of my babyhood. They could have seemed exuberant, insistent, frustrated, comical, even foreign—and yet they were my own first language.

WHERE THINGS HAVE NO NAME

In Lewis Carroll's *Through the Looking-Glass,* Alice comes to a wood "where things have no names."[42] She loses her own name and can't identify the trees or the fearless fawn that becomes her companion. Only when she regains her ability to give names to what surrounds her does she lose contact with the animal who had befriended her.

I am almost sure that the same bird, small and fearless, is arriving each morning to perch on the windowsill outside our bedroom. My neighbor, a serious birder, tells me he has identified 94 different species of birds in the courtyard of our apartment building. He confirms that there are fledglings, probably house sparrows, in a nest on our bedroom window sill. Sleepless, I listen to their infant babble, waiting for their voices to deepen, as my parents must have done with their children.

When I raise the window shade today, the mother bird flies to a nearby tree and emits a new stream of sounds. Almost involuntarily, I begin to tap on the window pane in imitation of the pattern of those sounds which I feel might be directed to me. Then a second bird suddenly appears, a companion or co-parent, and they fly out of sight together. I'm not sure which of us she had been signaling to, but she was teaching me about relationship in language of her own.

Long ago, when I lived where things had no name, I would have learned to communicate in new ways with fearless parents who were my companions to the very end of their lives.

---

42. Lewis Carroll, *Alice in Wonderland: Authoritative Texts of Alice's Adventures in Wonderland, Through the Looking-Glass, The Hunting of the Snark,* ed. Donald J. Gray, 2nd ed. (New York: W.W. Norton & Company, 1992), 135.

LIFE LIST

During a July afternoon walk in New Haven, David and I spotted a small yellow bird as it flew past us and into a neighboring yard. Knowing almost nothing about birds, I looked through my mother's well-thumbed copy of Roger Tory Peterson's *A Field Guide to the Birds,* hunting for a yellow-colored bird. I decided that we had seen an American Goldfinch (or perhaps a male Common Goldfinch, or, since i had been a cold spring and cool early summer, maybe a misinformed winter bird, the Eastern Goldfinch or the Yellow Warbler, the Redpull or the Siskin).

What I didn't hear was the voice of the goldfinch, presented by Peterson as "song, long-sustained, clear, light, and canary-like. In fligh each dip is often punctuated by a simple *ti-dee-di-di.*"[43] Had there beer a song, my mother would have heard it and identified it immediately. inherited her small whistle-like device that mimics bird sounds but have never used it, not knowing how to identify what it might attract.

I casually turn from Peterson's descriptions of yellow birds to a page headed "My Life List." Here, in small handwritten check marks, my mother has noted all the birds she has seen in her lifetime. How many there are, and how few are known to me.[44] In her list appear birds like Roseate Spoonbill, Limpkin, Purple Gallinule, Sanderling, Flicker, as well as the Solitary Sandpiper—but "Solitary" is crossed out. Peterson lists fifteen different sandpipers. The Solitary Sandpiper is distinguished by its "dark wings, [and] conspicuous white sides to the tail."[45] I see that my mother notes only what she can confirm, as she does in the list of my early vocabulary.

The robin and mockingbird receive a slanted ink mark rather than a penciled check. I wonder if these inked marks are my father's additions to my mother's Life List, noting familiar birds that could be seen and heard often near our Virginia house and that he wanted included in my mother's more far-ranging list.

---

43. Roger Tory Peterson, *A Field Guide to the Birds* (Boston: Houghton Mifflin 1947), 225.
44. The unbelievably popular mobile game, Pokémon Go, "is, in essence, digitally enhanced bird-watching. Find fantastic creatures like Weedle and Golbat in the wild, collect as many as possible, and get personal satisfaction and bragging rights from doing so." David Streitfeld, "Chasing Pokémon In Search Of Reality in a Game," *New York Times,* July 22, 2016, B1.
45. Peterson, 98.

Right before Towhee, Slate-colored Junco, and Song Sparrow, Goldfinch is marked by an inked slanted line that somehow curls up at the lower left corner, like a check mark, as if in anticipation of a daughter's finally seeing what both her parents see.

These handwritten notes give no indication of chronology. Which bird was identified first (though robin would be a likely guess) is unknown, like the word I first uttered. My mother will not claim she saw a "Solitary Sandpiper," only a sandpiper. She or my father crosses out "D.-C." [Double-Crested] in the listing of Cormorant. With the exception of the dingy Mexican Cormorant, my mother might have spotted any one of these dark water-birds. When accurate identification of what is seen or heard is not possible, none is given in either the Life List or the record of my first vocabulary.

I look now at a handwritten addition of Cattle Egret to Peterson's list. There is a penciled note in my mother's hand: what I first thought was "Fla. Graveyard Park" (my maternal grandparents are buried in Florida), under a magnifying glass turns out to be "Fla. Greynolds Park," a 249-acre park in North Miami Beach, Florida. Cattle Egrets are tropical herons found in warm parts of the southern United States (like Florida) and can also be spotted standing atop cows and horses in agricultural areas near wetlands.

Peterson has not listed or identified the Cattle Egret. He does, however, illustrate and briefly describe the yellow-*footed* Snowy Egret. Next to "yellow feet" in Peterson's book is a penciled note in my father's hand: "Cattle Egret—yellow bill, yellow leg." On their many trips to Florida, my parents must have seen a short, thick-necked egret with yellow feet—*and yellow bill*, a bird that found its way to North America in the 1950s but not into my mother's earlier edition of Peterson's *A Field Guide to the Birds.*

Here they are again, together—my parents meticulously creating a list based on their joint noticing of the living creature in their midst and each other's observations of that singular being.

DRONGO

Watching a documentary on the Kalahari in southwest Africa,
I see something my mother could never have witnessed. A drongo's
bird language alerts a family of meerkats to run for cover from a nearby
predator. The drongo then produces a different bird call recognized by
the meerkats as the "all clear" signal, and they immediately emerge from
their burrow. Like the mysterious communication between the
honeyguide and the Yao people of Mozambique, the interspecies
negotiation between a drongo and a group of meerkats is not explained
The documentary simply shows how the clever drongo, after winning
the trust of the meerkats, sounds a false alarm, and, as they scurry off,
swoops down to steal their prey[46] (possibly the thick wormlike larva of
beetles and other insects).

Some animals, of course, are capable from an early age of learning
how to communicate with others of their own species. Peter Marler, an
animal behaviorist, proposed that

> the drive to learn new things was an adaptive trait—and. . ..
> animals and humans both had it in their genes. Once
> triggered, individuals' capacity to fulfill these drives
> depended on nurturing and other environmental factors.

Marler demonstrated that some songbirds "not only learned their
songs, but also learned to sing in a dialect peculiar to the
region in which they were born."[47]

All this makes sense.

But the African Drongo has learned to sing in a "dialect"
peculiar to another species. Charles Darwin "thought that speech migh
have evolved from singing: `primeval man, or rather some early
progenitor of man, probably first used his voice in producing true
musical cadences, that is, in singing. . .. It is, therefore, probable that
the imitation of musical cries by articulate sounds may have given rise
to words expressive of various complex emotions.'"[48]

Perhaps in my infanthood I too "sang" in a dialect peculiar to a
species not yet recognized as my own.

---

46. "Planet Earth: Africa—`Kalahari,'" narrated by David Attenborough, BBC
America, July 14, 2015, 9-10 p.m.
47. Paul Vitello, "Peter Marler, Graphic Decoder of Birdsong, Dies at 86," *New
York Times*, July 28, 2014, A18.
48. Corballis, 145-146.

WHISTLING

There is a whistled form of speech among villagers in the mountains of northeastern Turkey, as well as in many other places. Whistled speech can be heard, and deciphered, over a distance of up to 5,000 meters—further than shouted speech. The skill is usually taught soon after a child learns to talk. Well, I don't know how much shouting I was prone to shortly after I learned to talk, but I wonder if I could have been adept at whistled speech, an alternative form of language that involves air swirling in tiny vortices at the edges of the lips.[49] I might have presented my early vocabulary in a way that was idiosyncratic, not likely to be recorded, even if someone happened to be listening.

Now I read about singers in Siberia who are able to produce many tones at once, including whistling.[50] This I think would have been beyond my capabilities. Or maybe not.

---

49. Julien Meyer, "The Whistled Sound," *Scientific American*, vol. 316, no. 2 (February 2017), 65, 64.
50. Jon Pareles, "Chasing His Muse, at the Genetic Level," *New York Times*, January 22, 2017, AR14.

THE LAST UNIVERSAL COMMON ANCESTOR

As I search for a personal linguistic ancestor (my own first word), I encounter the unresolved debate about a universal ancestor of all living beings. One candidate is a single-cell organism known as Luca, the Last Universal Common Ancestor, who may have lived some four billion years ago.[51] This merely intensifies the debate between those who think life began, as Charles Darwin did, in land-based pools and those who believe life originated in deep sea vents.

If we can't come to certainty about the workings of our own brains, or the miracle of human language itself, or the origins of a baby's developing vocabulary, it seems unlikely that we will easily resolve the mystery of life emerging on this planet. When answers simply provoke more questions, I am not complaining.

51. Nicholas Wade, "Meet Luca, Ancestor of All Living Things," *New York Time* July 26, 2016, D1. Chemist John Sutherland comments that "[the] portrait of Luca is 'all very interesting, but it has nothing to do with the actual origin of life.'" Ibid., D6.

A DEAD SALMON

In trying to understand the brain I brought with me at birth and its continuing development, I have been reading the work of neuroscientists. What some experts claim to be a milestone in neuroscience is a new map of the brain, presenting nearly 100 previously unknown regions. Dr. Matthew F. Glasser, a neuroscientist at Washington University School of Medicine, and his team recorded and studied high-resolution images of the brains of 1,200 volunteers. David C. Van Essen and his colleagues revisited a previously neglected patch in the brain, which they call 55b, that "becomes unusually active when people listen to stories."

Aha! One of the greatest mysteries in all of nature is about to be unfolded. I can now become more acquainted with 55b, a part of the language network in the brain that would have been extremely active in my life as a baby. Dr. Van Essen adds: "We shouldn't expect miracles and easy answers. . .but we're positioned to accelerate progress."[52]

Then I read that a "deliberately provocative paper, published in 2009, found apparent activity in the brain of a dead salmon." Anders Eklund and his team at Linkoping University in Sweden reveal that "the computer programs used by fMRI [functional magnetic resonance imaging] researchers to interpret what is going on in their volunteers' brains appear to be seriously flawed."[53]

The working of the human brain was comically challenged by a salmon! A dead salmon.

---

52. Carl Zimmer, "In Brain Map, Gears of Mind Get Rare Look," *New York Times*, July 21, 2016, A1, A17.
53. "Computer Says: Oops," *The Economist*, vol. 420, no. 8998 (July 16, 2016), 65. See also Kate Murphy, "Do You Believe in God, or Is That a Software Glitch?" *New York Times*, August 28, 2016, SR5.

YOUR BRAIN DOESN'T KNOW HOW OLD IT IS

I am no longer surprised by the speculations of various members of the scientific community. In fact, I think I often find myself nodding in agreement with de Waal: "I am not sure that I think in words."[54] But now I read Ian Tattersall's startling description of "the spontaneous invention of language":

> One can readily imagine—at least in principle—
> how a group of hunter-gatherer children in
> some dusty corner of Africa began to attach
> spoken names to objects and feelings, giving
> rise to a feedback loop between language and
> thought. This innovation would then have rapidly
> spread through a population already biologically
> predisposed to acquire it.[55]

Can you readily imagine children as the ancient originators of the capacity for language that distinguishes our species from all others? If children, why not babies? "Your brain doesn't know how old it is," Pau Nussbaum says. "And what it wants to do is learn."[56]

54. de Waal, 101.
55. Ian Tattersall, "At the Birth of Language," *New York Review of Books*, vol. 5 no. 13 (August 18, 2016), 28.
56. Paul Nussbaum, quoted by Constance Gustke, "For Effective Brain Fitness Do More Than Play Simple Games," *New York Times*, July 9, 2016, B5. Wendy Suzuki, professor of neural science and psychology at New York University, ha said, "Every time you learn something new, the brain changes." Ibid.

EINSTEIN'S GENERAL THEORY OF RELATIVITY

Neuroscientists at Carnegie Mellon University believe that "thinking about physics prompts common brain-activation patterns. . .used for processing rhythm and sentence structure," brain responses that occur "in the same regions that activate when people watch dancers. . .. [and]listen to music. . .. These results suggest that general neural structures are repurposed for dealing with high-level science."[57]

To this day, I still have trouble with Einstein's theory of relativity and curved space and string theory. It is fascinating to know that when in my infancy I was responding to "rhythm" (which, I realize, must have been a lot of the time) or listening to music, inside and outside the womb, I was activating neural structures that might eventually allow me to succeed (just barely) in my first college course in physics.

My baby brain could have been preparing me for a future of challenges in learning new science. That is both reassuring and a little disheartening.

---

57. Jordana Cepelewicz, "Your Brain on Physics," *Scientific American*, vol. 315, no. 2 (August 2016), 15.

FORGETTING AND REMEMBERING

We don't, most of us, remember much about our very early life, including the moment we entered it. In trying to recover what memory will not disclose, what I have not considered is how the brain functions to remove certain memories, especially those we are quite willing to do without.

Neuroscientists at the University of Cambridge are studying a memory-control mechanism in the brain in order to see whether it is possible to train people in suppression. This research is intended to help those with post-traumatic stress disorder for whom suppressing certain negative memories might be a desirable skill. There is a catch. Actively trying to forget a specific memory could negatively affect general memory.

The phenomenon under study has been called an "amnesic shadow" because it seems to "block recollection of unrelated events happening around the time of decreased hippocampal activity." Some experts not involved in the study believe that the amnesic shadow might explain why some people "have poor memory of everyday events." The brain can, without our conscious interference, allow certain recollections. It might be trained to "halt the spontaneous retrieval of potentially painful memories."[58]

If I could be trained in the art of removing amnesic shadow, I might recover forgotten traces of my infanthood that were precious to my developing life.

---

58. Bahar Gholipour, "Can We Learn How to Forget?," *Scientific American*, vol. 315, no. 2 (August 2016), 17, 16.

HAIR

My hair, uncut for over seven months, is growing. It has the length and look of my mother's hair when I was a baby. I find a photo of me hugging a favorite animal, a stuffed rabbit wearing a long reversible dress that, unfurled, reveals another, upside-down rabbit wearing a similar dress. My hair, flying about underneath a thin headband, is surprisingly curly, just like now.

"Hair" is one of the words on the list. I touch my hair often in its new length. Its texture and softness remind me of my mother's hair which I touched long before and right after her death.

There are photographs of me as a baby touching many things: a nose, the inside of a mouth, hands and upper arms, my own fingers, the upper buttons of whatever blouse or shirt a parent was wearing, the plastic duck on my personal toilet seat, the wooden sides of my playpen, a glass of orange juice, a rattle, a Valentine someone must have given me, my father's knee and thigh, books I am scattering from a low bookcase, what looks like a grapefruit, the sides of a neighbor's stroller, an orange, a bottle of water, a small tree branch, the back of a striped lawn chair, the long handle of a mirror. But nobody's hair.

Did I learn the word "hair" by touching my mother's hair as she held me off-camera? Did I wonder why my father's hair looked and felt different? Did I have a doll with interesting hair that was unlike my own? Did I play with the ends of my hair as if it were one of my toys? Did I know that hair will keep growing if you don't cut it?

If I understood any of this, did it make a difference? Like so much in the list, "hair" is a mystery.

ZOOM

New strategies for human communication proliferate. Faces crowd together in small, squarish boxes on computer screens. Vocal sound and the movement of lips are usually not synchronous. Images freeze or disappear. Awkward gaps punctuate conversations.

And yet.

My nephew Robert organizes a videoconference on July 5th, a virtual gathering of 20 family members, ranging in age from two and a half to eighty-two. We will begin at 5:30 p.m. for those in Frankfurt and Leuven; 8:30 a.m. for those in Seattle; 9:30 a.m. for those in Denver; 11:30 a.m. for those in Connecticut, New Jersey, Maryland, and Virginia. Half of these relatives I have never seen, but here they all are, with no face masks and a fictive proximity to each other possible during the pandemic.

I am wary, not knowing what to say to distant relatives whose weddings I may have attended and with whom I now only exchange holiday cards or emails. The voices I remember are from a different time in our lives when we were younger, less burdened. I write, teach, conduct my professional life without loss of language. Now a family event asks for a speaking self transformed by technology.

My summer pandemic walks in New Haven have muted me in the presence of others. The unimaginable has become my new reality.

In the soundscape of my relatives' voices, I will find my way back to language and perhaps recapitulate the wonder of a child's joining an adult world talking to me.

A SWEET MINUTE

Two very small children bump up against each other repeatedly and then leap in the air simultaneously on their front porch while a mother sits on the grass, smiling, talking to a silent child in a black baby carriage. On my return, the baby has emerged wearing a long yellow dress. Her mother catches my eye, smiles at me, continues to croon in Spanish as the grandmother takes a photograph of them.

Earlier I "attend" my first virtual wedding, the second marriage, late in life, of the mother of a former student. About two dozen guests, all wearing protective masks in response to COVID-19, sit in the backyard of a Florida home. Like their guests, the elderly bride and groom are masked except when, for a sweet minute, to cheers of "Hallelujah," they kiss.

I do not enter either of these very differently languaged events, one virtual and the other in a language I do not speak. How different from my life as a baby: a world of words beckons and I do not try to respond.

ART MASKS: REMBRANDT

The Interfaith Volunteer Caregivers of Greater New Haven send me a black cloth face mask for use during the COVID-19 pandemic. A student's mother sends me a reversible, blue-flowered cloth mask and a plain brown one for David. On my daily walks I see a variety of homemade, brightly colored face masks, often fashioned from repurposed materials.

Gift shops at art museums undergoing financial hardship have been selling face masks featuring artwork. At the National Gallery's gift shop in London, they are among the biggest sellers since the Gallery reopened July 8, 2020. Anti-boredom mask designs pop up everywhere. The Metropolitan Museum of Art in New York, the Uffizi in Florence, the Klimt Villa in Vienna, and the Stedelijk art museum in Amsterdam offer a variety of masks that feature famous paintings.

Perhaps the most startling of these art masks is one sold at Amsterdam's Rijksmuseum: a wide-eyed self-portrait by Rembrandt. A face mask with a face is the kind of visual communication that an 18-month-old would probably appreciate.

THREE MOMENTS OF COGNITIVE DISSONANCE

On the grass near the curb, a huge green vase, about as tall as I was at 18 months, with a sign, "Free," flapping in the breeze. On the sidewalk, at an intersection, a new pair of brown and white woman's pumps, as if just about to step off into the street. On a small frontyard fence, a string of sparkling, multi-colored Christmas lights; behind them, on a short black pole, a sign: "Welcome, summer," with a picture of an orange beach chair, straw hat with pink bows, and gulls flying over a blue-green sea.

Even without knowing the words "Free," "Welcome," and "summer," as a baby unacquainted with the concept of cognitive dissonance, I think my response to these visual anomalies would have been wordless wonder and delight.

STRANGE THINGS (IN THE NEIGHBORHOOD)

Repeated hints of early afternoon thunder and darkening skies, but no rain—and no thunder. Men painting second- and third-floor windows in 90 degree heat. A woman complimenting the sound of a little boy's tricycle bell as she runs by. In somebody's backyard, a basketball hoop on a stand five feet high next to one three feet high. In what looks like pink lipstick on a car window: "Hotel Workers United." Diners served lunch in the parking lot of a restaurant. Standing in the middle of the sidewalk as I approach, a shirtless, middle-aged man in red shorts who coughs and says, "I am not sick."

On the grass, I see a blue, yellow, green and orange umbrella with pole and written message: "<u>Please note</u>. Beach umbrella <u>works</u> [underlined twice]. Just not able to disassemble/collapse pole." This would be the kind of meticulous message that my mother might have written, and that I would never have read. The only word I knew in that note was "please" which tells me something about the kind of language heard at home and tried out on my own.

*   *   *

What is strangest of all in the neighborhood, of course, are the pandemic masks that separate language from the physicality of speech by hiding the movements of the mouth, tongue, and lower face. Classical Greek and Japanese Noh theater, among others, used masks in performance, but in the new normal of masks in everyday life, actors and audience, those who speak and those who listen, are indistinguishable.

US

On the television show *This is Us*, a premature baby arrives, weighing under three pounds. A hospital nurse tells the parents they can talk or sing to make the infant more comfortable while she takes blood and urine samples. The nurse may have wanted to give the parents something to do or simply distract them from a procedure that might cause anxiety, but she is also implying that Jack, not even able to cry, could hear his parents' voices, just as he had in the womb. The father, who seems to have difficulty recognizing the tiny body enveloped in multiple tubes and devices that keep him alive and breathing, abruptly leaves the room. Jack's mother, who carried him inside her in a much reduced form, sings and talks to her baby. Later the father returns and is for the first time allowed to hold Jack in his arms. Suddenly his eyes light up and he communicates silently with his silent son.

I imagine my father holding a small baby in his arms, communicating without words, waiting patiently for more ways of being together to emerge. And I wonder now how many one-way conversations my mother and I had, and what she told me in those unrecoverable moments of my life before I could speak.

MOTHER'S DAY

Today is Mother's Day. Last evening on television I saw a fictional mother and daughter try to convince each other that they had both been ideal parents. The camera knew the truth. Time and time again, in between each exchange in their dialogue, a flashback informed us of imperfect mothering amid the stress and difficulty of new parenthood.

I must have been trouble to my young parents, but I can't remember any of that. Less than a year before my mother's death, I finally asked her if she enjoyed being a mother. She replied, "Oh, I loved it. I *never* for one moment regretted the decision, and. . .she was a *pretty* baby and a *darling* baby, and a *good* baby. There was nothing not to like."[59] But there must have been *something* not to like. And yet apparently my mother never told a lie in her life. When a boy in my 9th grade class who liked me phoned and asked if I was home, I told my mother to say that I was out. She wouldn't lie, so I stepped onto the back porch and waited in the pouring rain until she conveyed my message.

* * *

In today's *New York Times,* there is a two-page ad for Hunter College, my mother's alma mater. The headline says: "Mothers who went to Hunter College really do know best." Below that, I read that "[w]omen who went to Hunter College taught their children a love of learning and the desire to excel."[60] I know that, but there is much I would like to learn now about my Hunter College mother that no amount of learning can provide.

What both parents gave me, along with much else, are the wonders of language, language that wants and tries to reach beyond memory—and fails.

---

59. Susan Letzler Cole, *Missing Alice: In Search of a Mother's Voice* (Syracuse: Syracuse University Press, 2007), 117.
60. "Mothers who went to Hunter College really do know best," *New York Times,* May 12, 2019, N14-15.

LOST SELVES

"No wonder is ever quite equal to that first, speechless wonder—gazing at the mysterious individuals leaning over us unable yet to say *Who are you? Why do you care for me? What does it mean, that you care for me? What does it mean, we are here together? Only feed me, only love me forever.*" A few pages later in her memoir *The Lost Landscape*, Joyce Carol Oates reveals that her mother was *"given away"* when she was not yet a year old, because her mother's father had been killed in a tavern fight and the mother was too poor to support her new baby.

Writing in her mother's voice, Oates says:

> *There were ten children. I was the baby.*
> *I was born too late, I was the baby*
> *that our mother could not keep.*
> *My sisters and brothers did not miss me—*
>   *I think.*
> *They would have looked at me and tried to think why*
> *I was the one to be given away, and not them.*[61]

How very sad this is, and yet the baby, like every other, had its first moment of "speechless wonder" and unknowing. Answers would come later, or not at all, but the speechless gaze held.

Perhaps that first silent experience of wonder and mystery is a peak moment in our non-speaking lives. Maybe the search for our first word is a search for the beginning of a disappointment that only language can provide.

---

61. Joyce Carol Oates, *The Lost Landscape: A Writer's Coming of Age* (New York: HarperCollins, 2015), 325-326, 332. Oates writes, "Our lost selves are not really accessible." Ibid., 264.

BIRTH DAY

Today is my mother's birthday, once again.

Her 28th birthday, 19 days before she gave birth to me, would have passed without my notice. Maybe many birthdays did. I have a former student, now a dear friend, whose birthday is the same as hers, May 16. I'll call soon to congratulate him.

When was I able to say "happy birthday" to my mother? The words "birth" and "day" do not appear in my 200-word vocabulary. There is "baby" of course, but that would have been me, not her. My brother was born at home when I was three so maybe then I understood something about birth, but what? Once I knew that someone had to be born to be a baby, did I think that anyone who had a birthday was still baby?

At eighteen months, I could have said "here it is" or "ta ta" (thank you) on a birthday. I hope I did.

I probably thought that only my mother could have a birthday today.

A MILLIONTH OF A SECOND

A team of quantum physicists, using an IBM quantum computer, have reported that they sent a single, simulated elementary particle back to its own past by a millionth of a second. If this time-reversal process were ever able to be replicated and hastened in my lifetime (totally unlikely), I'd like to revisit a time I don't remember, when my parents were awakened by the inconvenient sounds of their baby. I know that at some point they instituted the practice, recommended by somebody, of letting us cry until my brother and I fell back to sleep on our own—which apparently didn't take that long.

As our parents lay awake, listening to their baby's tiny repertoire, her efforts at communication, did they notice a pattern, a change in tone, a sudden pause as if their child was listening back? And did I take pleasure in the sounds I discovered myself able to make, after so long a silence in the womb?

If I were able to reverse time and return to what I felt in such a moment, I would not have the language to express it.

MEDITATION ON BREATH

In my second week of meditation at the public library in New Haven, the teacher says, "Feel your breath in your body." Then, later: "Feel you breath in your whole body." It sounds so natural, but it isn't. When I was just born, when I took my first breath, did I feel my breath in my whole body? After all, that body wasn't very big and perhaps my breath found its way easily through every part. Every future breath may be an "illusion of the first time," the way actors recreate their roles on stage in each new performance.

I am told: "Keep your eyes open. Like your ears. They are open. They have no agenda." How hard this is for an adult and how natural it must have been in infancy.

Listening to my breathing, I travel back to my earliest life. What did my first breath feel like? Did it jolt me, wordlessly? Did I notice my first breath or did it pass outside my attention, like my first word?

"Notice your breath," I'm told in the meditation session. "Just observe it. There are no 'shoulds.' There are no 'wrongs.' Just stay in the moment."[62] It's hard to do, though as an infant I must have managed this most of the time.

Noticing is a legacy handed on, slowly and fitfully, and with some difficulty, to my adult life.

---

62. Lee Barbers, Meditation Leader, New Haven Free Public Library, September 27, 2016.

CHANTING MEDITATION

Without quite knowing what I was doing, I participated in various forms of meditation at the local Zen center in New Haven. Before the sitting meditation and the walking meditation, there is chanting. In the Foreword of a booklet with the transliterated text of Korean chants, Zen Master Seung Sahn writes:

Chanting meditation means keeping a not-moving mind and perceiving the sound of your own voice. Perceiving your voice means perceiving your true self or true nature. Then you and the sound are never separate....When you and the sound become one, you don't hear the sound, you are the sound.... Any sound will do.[63]

I don't know about the "not-moving mind," but this description of what is supposed to happen during the chanting meditation connects my adult experience with the first cry of babyhood. After the first sound, I and my own voice are never separate again.

"Any sound will do."

---

63. Seung Sahn, Foreword, *Chanting with English Translations and Temple Rules* (Cumberland, R.I.: Kwan Um School of Zen, 1996), v-vi.

IN PRAISE OF AIR

A poem by Simon Armitage ends: "My first word, everyone's first word, was air." My nephew Ben provided the following information. The poem, "printed on a 10m by 20m piece of material. . .coated with microscopic pollution-eating particles. . .capable of absorbing the pollution from 20 cars every day," was attached to a building at the University of Sheffield in the United Kingdom. This giant installation, unveiled in May of 2014, was said to have the capacity to remove harmful nitrogen oxides from 73,000 cars over a ten-year period. Ironically, a poem that begins, "I write in praise of air," was removed due to wind damage.[64]

My first "word" was air; that was probably all I could do. But not quite all. Michael Corballis reminds us that babies "can suckle and breathe at the same time." In contrast, as we grow older, we, "unlike other mammals, cannot breathe and swallow at the same time" since "breathing and swallowing. . .share the same passage" in the vocal tract.[65] To inhale and exhale is a trickier enterprise than it might seem. Babies can master this without thought or practice.

Speaking requires a certain degree of control over the air we breathe The poem that meant to speak in praise of air failed to control the movement of that colorless, odorless, tasteless, gaseous mixture that envelops the earth. To learn language is to learn how to negotiate the outward flow of breath that produces recognizable sounds of normal speech.

The baby's cry is the first use of air outside the womb.

I write in praise of air.

---

64. Simon Armitage, "In Praise of Air."
https://www.theguardian.com/books/2014/may/14/new-simon-armitage-poem-fights-pollution-roadside. Accessed June 2, 2016.
http://thetab.com/uk/sheffield/2014/11/04/in-praise-of-air-poem-is-blown-away-in-the-wind-4494. Accessed June 2, 2016. I am indebted to Benjamin Letzler for alerting me to these links.
In *Nutshell*, Ian McEwan's just-born narrator says: "I'm breathing. Delicious. My advice to newborns: don't cry, look around, taste the air." Ian McEwan, *Nutshell* (New York: Doubleday, 2016), 196.
65. Corballis, 142.

LOOKING AT A FACE LOOKING

Long ago I watched my mother greet her son and daughter-in-law bringing their infant to her home for a visit. After the baby was placed on a blanket for delighted inspection, my brother happened to mention that his son ate like a bird. My mother did not respond to her son, but sat near her grandchild, looking directly at him as she carefully explained in detail the hard lives of birds who spend a great deal of time foraging for food and materials for their nests. The baby gazed back at his grandmother, an inveterate birdwatcher, with a deeply serious look on his listening face. I was struck by what seemed to be a dialogue between two faces looking steadily at each other.

Babies prefer to look at a face looking toward them rather than at one looking away, as Alexandra Horowitz acknowledges:

> Later, this mutual gazing between oneself
> and others will be a way to convey a sense
> of closeness or understanding. Indeed, the
> easiest way to get an infant to smile is to
> simply let them see you looking right at them.[66]

But Robert wasn't smiling. In that moment he seemed to be paying the kind of intense attention he now invests in any face-to-face adult conversation.

I think about the new words he was hearing, delivered in my mother's uniquely melodious voice. That mutual gaze, two sets of eyes looking at a face looking, marked a baby's listening to the beauty of speech.

---

66. Alexandra Horowitz, *On Looking: Eleven Walks with Expert Eyes* (New York: Scribner, 2013), 84. She adds: "It's not you, alas: any egg shape with eye shapes within it that you show to an infant will elicit coos and smiles of delight." Ibid.

TOOLS

Researchers can now show that "it's possible to listen to the structure of a protein [in the human body] as a melody, as it turns, twists, flattens and folds like a wild hair."[67] Were my movements in the womb wordless melodies waiting for the moment when my first breath became sound?

It has long been known, and documented, that certain nonhuman animals use tools. The capuchin monkeys of Serra da Capivara National Park in Brazil use rocks to dig or to crack open nuts. Scientists have reported that they also "spend time banging stones together, for no clear reason, producing sharp-edged flakes that are just like some of the first tools of early humans." The monkeys "have not grasped the idea of using those sharp flakes as potential tools."[68]

I have seen color photos of some of these non-utilitarian, sharp-edged stone flakes. The stones are quite lovely, even arresting. Could it be that the monkeys create sounds (banging) that simply please in the moment of their making? In our early life as infants, the sounds we utter may not serve any discernible purpose other than to have arrived in our midst. Adults, of course, often need to make babies' self-delighting babble utilitarian. But perhaps, like the capuchin monkeys of Brazil, infants are interested not so much in potential tools as in producing wordless melodies we bring into the world.

---

67. Joanna Klein, "Want to Identify Proteins? Just Listen," *New York Times*, October 25, 2016, D2.
68. James Gorman, "These Monkeys Make Tools, but Don't Use Them," *New York Times*, October 25, 2016, D2.

OPEN ALL THE TIME

"The human ear is open all the time; it has no lid to naturally refresh the auditory scene," Alexandra Horowitz writes. "But while our ears are always open, we only half attend to sounds they carry, given the racket coming from within our own heads." In addition to the "sounds of the placenta, the gurgle of intestines, and the coursing of. . .[the mother's] blood around the womb," before we are born we attend involuntarily to the sounds of speech we do not yet understand: the songs of birds; the hum of traffic; the sound of a chair falling. As adults, Horowitz reminds us, "attention is an intentional, unapologetic discriminator."[69] Not so for the languageless, mainly sightless being just about to be born. Inside the womb we might be the best listeners we will ever be.

The proliferation of smartphones and other technological offerings, as we develop from children to teenagers to adults, makes us less open to the auditory and visual world that surrounds us. As infants, probably the first thing we ask is: "what's that?" Those words are on the list of my vocabulary at eighteen months. Horowitz points out that identifying what we have spotted as a baby "gets us no closer to understanding. . ., but it is often taken as a stand-in for that understanding." Even to be taught to name what we hear does not help us to fully engage the world. What might is the ability to be open all the time: to "hear beyond. . .names,"[70] as we once did.

---

69. Alexandra Horowitz, *On Looking*, 213, 212, 12.
70. Ibid., 214.

CATEGORIES

It is true that the "use of language cannot change reality, but it can change the perception of reality."[71] A friend's young son calls me "Auntie Susan." He has two parents, grandparents, several uncles and aunts. I am a female adult offering affection and interest and "auntie" seems the right approximate category for my role in his life.

Gary Lubyan and Benjamin Bergen claim that

> Language. . .plays an important and sometimes critical role in learning to selectively represent items in a way that promotes their categorization . . . . Around the age of 2, humans transition from being merely trainable to something qualitatively more powerful—being *programmable*. We can sculpt the minds of others into arbitrary configurations.[72]

My eighteen-month-old vocabulary includes the word "auntie," with no accompanying proper noun. I had several biological aunts, all living at some distance and not visiting frequently in my early life. A female adult attending to me daily with affection and interest in my early life appears in the list as "ulain," my version of the name of the African-American maid who took care of me while my parents were at work during the day.

What "programmable" categorization would *ulain* inhabit in my young mind? Into what "arbitrary configuration" would she eventually be sculpted? In my babyhood I may have freely created particular relationships while language lagged behind, waiting for its future role of reprogramming the mind. Lubyan and Bergen suggest that "we can conceive all sorts of things for which we lack names or linguistic expressions."[73]

Ulain could have been my "auntie."

---

71. P.R. Hays, quoted by Gary Lupyan, "The Centrality of Language in Human Cognition" (2015), 14. http://sapir.psych.wisc.edu/papers/lupyan_CentralityOf Language. pdf. Accessed July 11, 2016.

72. Gary Lupyan and Benjamin Bergen, "How Language Programs the Mind," *Topics in Cognitive Science* (2015),5,2. http://sapir.psych.wisc.edu/ papers/lupyan_bergen_2015.pdf. Accessed July 11, 2016. These views have been called in question by Chaz Firestone and Brian J. Scholl, "Cognition does not affect perception; Evaluating the evidence for 'top-down effects'" (2015). http://perception.research.yale.edu/preprints/Firestone-Scholl-BBS.pdf. Accessed July 12, 2016.

73. Lubyan and Bergen, Ibid., 13, n.4.

DIFFERENCES

I overhear someone say that babies can't distinguish gender. That seems at once startling and obvious. What if my parents had twins and bathed my brother and me together. Would his penis set him permanently apart or would it be something that could change with time or could be eventually given over to me or would I really notice or care at all about it? If I saw my parents naked, would I have known that my body would later look like only one of them (and which one)? When they held me pressed against their chests, did I register the different shapes of their bodies as indicating differences that outlasted their contact with me?

At first, everything would have been somewhat alien, like the newly unobstructed sounds of adult voices. I was no longer having my life inside another body; I was on my own and yet not on my own. I might have been too busy figuring out this non-womb world to worry about sexual or racial differences while male and female, white and black, hands dressed and undressed me, fed me, cleaned me.

In the list of my vocabulary at eighteen months, I see evidence that gender at some point perhaps entered my world: "auntie" and "uncle," "gmama" and "papa," "daddy" and "mama" (did I know that one was male and the other was female?). There are also "man," "boy," "good girl." And there is "Susan." Did "baby" (also one of my early words) have no gender until it became a man or a boy, an uncle or a grandma? Was Susan ever going to be a boy or was a boy ever going to be another Susan? As a baby, what did I understand about gender differences?

What is most alien right now is that I have no language for this beautiful unknowing.

CHIMERA

Apparently, microchimerism has been going on for hundreds of millions of years in mammals' reproduction, but I just found out about it. I wonder if my mother knew that not too long after my conception, her cells and mine were part of two-way traffic across the placenta. Microchimerism extended what Katherine Rowland calls this "silent chemical conversation" between my mother and me for years after my birth. In fact, my fetal cells could have been found in her "bloodstream, skin, and all major organs, even showing up in [her] beating heart." My fetal cells could have decreased her risk of Alzheimer's, rheumatoid arthritis, and some kinds of cancer (though not the one that killed her). It is also possible that microchimeric cells "boost the mother's tolerance of successive pregnancies, representing an 'altruistic act of first children' to support the success of their genetically similar offspring."[74] This is astonishing and moving. Did I begin to help my mother and younger brother even before I was born?

If my mother and I shared cells, does that change who we were?

I don't think so.

* * *

The importance of being noticed, thrown forward more than seven decades, is met by my noticing back. That is another kind of microchimerism.

---

74. Katherine Rowland, "We Are Multitudes." https://aeon.co/essays/microchimerism-how-pregnancy-changes-the-mothers very-dna. Jan. 11, 2018. Accessed June 18, 2018. Microchimera takes its name from the chimera, a mythological female creature, the composite of a lion, goat, and serpent.

SEVENTY-EIGHT

I reached the same age my mother was when she died: 78. I like the sound of that number. Maybe just the sound. I wonder when I first put two numbers together—possibly one and one, or one and two. First, of course, I would have *heard* numbers. Perhaps my parents were counting my toes for me, or quoting a song or story they both knew, or referring to a trip we were to take with relatives or friends. Certainly I would have seen more than one person or chair or tree as a baby, but what did I know about addition. Multiplication evades me even today.

Did I often eavesdrop inadvertently on my parents' talking about numbers of persons or events or messes without ever knowing what I was hearing?

Did I know that numbers even referred to more than one thing?

When did I know that together my hands or feet made two, but not my fingers or toes?

If my parents sang happy birthday to me when I was one year old (I'm sure they did), how could I know that I wouldn't ever be one year old again?

As an adult I attended the birthday party of a friend's two-year-old daughter. When we sang, "Happy birthday to you," Sarah kept repeating "to." She knew how old she was but a preposition had become a number. So when exactly did numbers enter my own early life?

I try to remember a time when 78 was just a number I didn't know.

I think I am learning that the sound of a number might be what matters most again.

NUMBERS

Thanks to the coronavirus, I find myself looking more and more closely at what ought to be a familiar neighborhood. Yesterday I noted the dates 1816-1903 carved into the pinkish-brown stone near the startlingly orange door of The First Baptist Church of New Haven. In my new state of watchful apprehension of who is just behind, ahead, or approaching me during my daily walks, I also noticed that a nearby church was over two hundred years old.

There are only two numbers in the list of my first 200 words. Just "two" and "three." I see "toes" on the list, but did I count them by stopping and starting again after "two" or after "three"? My brother was not yet born. Did "two" refer to both of my parents, or to me and one of them; did "three" refer to all of us? Perhaps these numbers were only used to refer to things I wanted or owned or wanted to own.

Certainly I could not have known that the year was 1940 or 1941—or even what such numbers meant. I wouldn't have been in awe of a building over two hundred years old. I probably didn't even know how old I was and certainly not how old my parents were. It seems that I was satisfied living in a world with a number no larger than three. That seems to be all that was needed.

PART 2: WORDS

A SMALL WOODEN TABLE

I wonder where in their small apartment my parents recorded their list of my first vocabulary. There was no obvious place. Beyond the kitchen was a dining alcove that opened into the living room. There were two bedrooms, as I recall, and a bathroom.

Emily Dickinson wrote 1,800 poems on a small wooden table, 17 3/8ths inches square. My parents probably didn't need much space for the recording of a list, but where did they do it—and what difference would it make if I knew?

Maybe if they wrote in the living room or in the dining alcove or even in the kitchen, that might suggest the kinds of words I was most likely to hear, directed at particular objects in particular places—or maybe not. My first vocabulary could have been worked on when they were outdoors or reading aloud my favorite books or glimpsing a bird outside the window. Still, if I could imagine my parents with their baby daughter, writing on a tiny table 17 3/8ths inches square, I would feel so much closer to my earliest speaking self, the self that first delighted in a shared language.

SNOW

In a poem by Robert Pinsky, a mother shows her baby snow falling outside the window of their home. She is trying to teach her child to talk:

> *Snow* she said, *Snow,* and you opened your small
>   brown fist
>   . . .to hold the reflection
> Of torches and faces inside the window glass
> And through it. . ..
>   the motion
> Of motes and torches that at her word you reached
> Out for, where you were, it was you, that
>   bright confusion.[75]

Snow is not in my 200-word infant vocabulary. I thought it might have been there but it wasn't. There is also no word with an "s" followed by an "n." Perhaps that is a sequence of sounds I wasn't able to make yet. I would have seen snow before I was a year old (it snowed lightly in the winters of 1940 and 1941) and it might have interested me.

How complicated it must have been to identify objects and events for the first time. Perhaps I attempted to grasp in my hand images reflected in the glass of our window as my mother talked to me, trying to turn a winter scene into language. "[A]t her word," did I, without speaking, reach out for "that bright confusion" of snow and myself?

---

75. Robert Pinsky, "Window," in *The Want Bone* (New York: Ecco Press, 1990), ll. 20, 21-23, 26-28, p. 9.

WORD MAGIC

The husband of a dear friend died of multiple organ failure in New York City during the pandemic. For months she and I did not speak his name. During a recent telephone conversation, my friend mentions a laptop I had given her long ago which she has now replaced after her husband told her it was too old and too slow. Agreeing with his advice, I repeated his name.

Suddenly I felt an electric shock: he was there, real, present.

And I wonder if this was my childhood experience of what words were meant to do.

WHITE BUTTERFLIES

In the backyard garden below our third-floor window is a baby, wearing only a diaper, held high in her father's arms, one hand curled around his shoulder and the other excitedly pointing in the direction of shiny black eggplants, just ripening tomatoes, and vines attached to makeshift poles, former tree branches that had fallen after the last Connecticut storm. Suddenly I realize that the Chinese father and his baby are following a solitary white butterfly across the lawn. They move slowly, the daughter making unintelligible sounds as the father bends his head close to his child, murmurs a response and points toward the slowly moving butterfly just ahead. On their return across the lawn, more and more white butterflies appear, but now, as they fly past her, the baby turns her attention to the garden.

And I wonder if my own father ever took his baby daughter for a survey of the backyard lawn before he and my mother left for work—and what I was saying to him then that is unrecoverable now.

MOTHER'S FIRST WORD

Watching a rerun of an old TV show, I see a woman give birth to a baby girl. It is a difficult birth, with audible agonized cries of the mother followed by the sudden wail of her child as she takes her first breath. A male relative who had attended the birth says, rather giddily, "Hi, baby." The new mother bends her head to kiss the head of the baby who has been placed on her chest. Her first word, whispered close to an ear that has never before heard her mother's voice outside the womb, is the baby's name, "Nora."

I have been unable to discover the first word I ever said. What was the first word I *heard*? Was it my own name? My parents' voices outside the womb would be both recognizable and new. No longer buffered by the walls of the uterus, close by, the first word that reached my new ears—though I did not know it then—would have introduced me to the world.

FARBLONGET

My brother writes me, humorously, while reading my book:

> I recall our mother sometimes referring
> to something with a funny-sounding word that
> I heard as furblunget. I never heard
> anyone else use that word, and kind of
> thought she had made it up. . ..
> Until this morning, when I ran across a
> website on Yiddish words that included
> farblonget, defined variously as "bludgeoned,
> beaten down," or as "lost, dysfunctional,
> bewildered, confused."
> There is a good chance that farblonget was your
> first word.[76]

I learn later that I may discard "bludgeoned," "beaten down," and "dysfunctional" as translations of farblonget. "The word is almost always used in the sense of someone who is hopelessly lost, literally or figuratively, someone who has just lost their way. . ..bewildered, confused, mixed up would all apply."[77]

Ken's memory, I admit, has always outdistanced my own. I don't remember this word at all. But why not *farblonget?* One more missing word on the list. When you get right down to it, wouldn't I have been farblonget even then?

---

76. Kenneth Letzler, email correspondence, June 23, 2018.
77. Sara Brzowsky, email correspondence, July 5, 2018.

MA, MA, MA

Eight hours after giving birth by C-section to quadruplets, children she and her husband Carlos had been hoping to have for many years, Erica Morales died of hypovolemic shock before she had a chance to hold her babies. Erica's mother Sondra, who had been asked to move in temporarily to help with childcare, remained in the house with her son-in-law, becoming a daytime surrogate parent after their father returned to full-time work when the quadruplets were seven months old.

Although the babies do not yet understand that they have lost their mother, Carlos "frequently shows them pictures of. . .[Erica] and displays photos of her throughout their home." Of the four babies, "Tracy was the first to talk. Her first words at 10 months—Ma, Ma, Ma—were 'a shock,' says Carlos. 'It was very hard to hear Tracy say that. I looked at Sondra and she started crying. It was a good moment, but at the same time it was sad.'"[78]

Ma, ma, ma. Did Tracy, more than her siblings, respond to the sound of her grandmother's grieving voice as she spoke to the babies about their deceased mama? Did Tracy feel that since other words, like "juice," were followed by the appearance of something that seemed connected to a sound she heard, a mama would also appear at some point? Perhaps Tracy simply liked hearing this word spoken with love by the woman who so attentively cared for her, despite her mourning. Maybe she was actually saying *mama,* and then repeating the beginning of a sound she didn't understand but enjoyed producing. Maybe her grandmother was *ma, ma, ma,* her baby language for *grandma*, a word she probably heard a lot. And, of course, maybe Tracy's first word was lost in the interstices of loving caretaking, as mine was.

Amid the visual images of the mother she literally never saw or felt, Tracy's words call out to the woman who had given her life. Brian Henry writes in his poem, "Elegy Elegy":

How thin is the human voice,
it cannot keep even the dead
distant, on the other side of any
thing we would call any thing.[79]

---

78. Caitlin Keating and Nicole Weisensee Egan, "Life Without Mom," *People,* March 7, 2016, 56-57.
79. Brian Henry, "Elegy Elegy," *New York Times Magazine,* May 29, 2016, 17.

IMMIGRANTS

There is a lot more talk about immigrants after the 2016 election of the President of the United States and its aftermath. Moving along the birth canal, with our mothers' help, we are all immigrants, finding an opening to a foreign world. How could it be otherwise? In our first infancy, we have no understanding of the culture, the values, the language, even the look and taste and smell of our new landscape. We could not pass a test of citizenship, nor is it clear that we know right from wrong. We have no sense of fashion, could possibly be accused of indecent exposure, shamelessly beg for food and physical comfort. Our life from its very beginnings is an immigrant's story.

What would I want to bring into my new life? I think it would be words. In fact, I wonder, if I only had room for one word in my immigrant's suitcase, what it would be. I try to imagine that word.

I consider many possibilities as I comb through the list of 200 words. How innocent they seem. The word I want is not there.

Help.

DID I MISS YOU?

A friend writes me about a talk she had with her two young daughters, one six years old and the other three and a half.

> We were talking about when Violet was
> first in my belly, where we lived and
> what we did, and Mina said, "But where
> was I?" And I told her she wasn't
> anywhere yet. And she asked, "Did I
> miss you?" And I said yes.[80]

And so I wonder, when I wasn't anywhere yet, did I miss my mother any more than I do now?

---

80. Jillian Raucci Bedell, email correspondence, April 17, 2018.

LOVE

Which of my 200 words did I hear in the womb? I might have heard "baby" and "doctor." Did I hear someone say "push" before I spilt forth? Did anyone say "kiss" before my just-born self received it? (This I imagine; there is no mention in The *Child's Development and Health Record* of my first kiss.)

The journey from voicelessness in the womb to voicing outside it includes the silent taking in of the incomprehensible. Where does the incomprehensible lodge? Certain repeated words perhaps made no impression while others gradually acquired intelligibility. And when a particular sound "took," was it because of repetition, usefulness, simple mimicry, a little bit of luck? Was I in some sense nourished by sound itself—my sentient connection with the world outside?

I revisit the derivation of the word "infant" in my mother's beloved, old Latin dictionary: "**infans**: *not speaking, that cannot speak, without speech, mute, speechless.*"[81] In her novel, Elissa Ellott imagines Eve's first utterance to Adam in Paradise:

> I heard my voice, like an echo, and it
> confounded me for a moment. *What was this*
> *flow of breath that formed itself into odd,*
> *staccato sounds*? How strange it felt![82]

This fictional portrayal of the first woman's awakening to her own voice suggests how a baby might hear her own first utterance.

It would be a great surprise to breathe, to emit sounds, when before had no voice. In the womb I have lungs but no respiratory system that works on its own. My mother's blood breathes life into my fetal self, *inspires* (from the Latin: to breathe in) that life. Of course, none of these crucial words makes the list: not "blood" nor "breath" nor "life" nor "voice." Not even "word" is one of my 200 words!

I notice, with inappropriate shock, that "love" is also not on the list, and yet it must have surrounded me during almost every waking hour in the presence of my young parents. I would have heard that word over and over before I was a year and a half. Perhaps "love" meant being held when I said "up"; sung to when I said "cuckoo"; read to when I said "book"; given an apple, a banana, cereal, grapes, milk, orange juice, or toast when I said those words. Maybe "love" meant eyes, now fully open, gazing at eyes gazing back and sound pointedly directed at me in

81. Charlton T. Lewis, *A Latin Dictionary for Schools* (New York: American Book Company, 1916), 515.
82. Elissa Elliott, *Eve* (New York: Bantam Books, 2010), 33.

response to sounds I myself now made. Maybe "love," at the instant of its arrival, meant simply that I was noticed, enveloped with care: the invisible nurturing in the womb made visible and audible became love.

*   *   *

In the vocabulary of my infanthood, there is no "I" but everything revolves around it. In a sense, this is revolting; in another sense, it is exhilarating. Without money, job skills, education, status in society, sex appeal, elected office, I was the center of my 200-word world.

TUMMY

An actress, Jessica Alba, pregnant with her second child, says that her three-year-old daughter asks if she has "a baby in [her] tummy," and she replies, "Yes, but it'll be complicated."[83] "Tummy" is one of my 200 words at eighteen months. Eighteen months later, another baby, my brother, will emerge from my mother's tummy at home when no hospital beds are available. How complicated was that? Would my sense of "tummy" undergo a jolt? Would I wonder if my tummy too had a baby in it—and if not, why not? Would I want another tummy to have the next baby? Would I even *want* tummies to do that?

But at eighteen months none of this occurs to me. A tummy might ache a little or protrude. I might notice with occasional interest the cleaning of my bellybutton, without seeing it as the mark of my earlier lifeline.

"Tummy" would just have been a funny word to say. It is now. Then it may have sounded a little like, at least it rhymed with, "ti ti," my attempt at "toidy" (which I assume was toilet). I imagine myself rehearsing rhymes—or strings of alliteration, like "tip toe," "see-saw," "tick tock"—or repetitive alliterative rhyming (with occasional attempted onomatopoeia, like "choo choo," "kack kack" [duck], "moo moo"): "row, row," "night-night," "oh-oh," "hop, hop," "ta ta"(thank you), "rock, rock," "bye-bye." How many there are.

How many more there might have been—unvoiced, unrecorded.

---

83. "Getting Ready for Baby with. . .Jessica Alba," *People*, August 15, 2011, 94.

NOUNS ON THE MOVE

Nouns that prepare us for meeting our own body or another body have an action in mind. We meet ourselves and others simultaneously with help from language. The easiest words for babies to learn are not verbs but concrete nouns. But to what extent did I, does any baby, use nouns as verbs? Shakespeare's Cleopatra tells the women who accompany her at the end of her life: "[Caesar] words me, girls, he words me"; Gloucester's son Edgar says, "[King Lear] childed as I fathered!"[84] The nouns *child, father,* and (sadly) *word* are not on the list of my first 200 words but other nouns used as verbs may have inaugurated my lifelong interest in shifts in grammatical function. Words that refer to food and drink (*apple, banana, cereal, cheese, cracker, cup, egg, fruit, grape, jello, milk, orange, orange juice, toast, water*) or clothing (*bib, bow, coat, dress, gloves, hanky, hat, pocket, socks, shoes*) or means of entertainment (*ball, beads, bells,* possibly *block, choo choo* [train], *cuckoo* [song book], *dance, doll, mouse* [Mickey Mouse toy], *music, soldier* [bear], *toys*) might easily be spoken as requests or demands for action. Words that refer to locomotion (*bus, car, carriage, trolley*) or location (*bridge, chair, door, grass, house, out/outside, street*), like the adverbs *up* and *down*, could express a desire for movement, with imperative verbs missing. Words related to persons or animals (*auntie, baby, bear, birdie, bow wow* [dog], *boy, daddy, Danny, doctor, gmama* [grandma], *good girl* [if myself, not always accurate], *goose, he, horse, kack-kack* [duck], *kitty, mama, man, moo moo* [cow], *papa* [grandpa], *otto* (if this is a person), *Ricky, Susan, Ulain, uncle*) might function as pointers (pointing being an early method of communication) but also as expressions of a present, past, or future need for physical presence.

What was perhaps frequently used (*bandage, bath, bed, book, box, broom, brush, comb, cotton,* [tooth]*paste, piece, rag* [washcloth], *soap, ti ti* [toidy], *tick tock* [clock], *toothbrush*); often visible (*dark, leaf, light, money, moon, paper, penny, tree, wall*); or quite audible (*king cole* [sung], possibly *kiss, noise, music, pussy, row row* [sung]) could have been asked for or protested against; sung, nouns or noun phrases would already create an action.

---

84. William Shakespeare, *Antony and Cleopatra*: 5.2.187; *King Lear*: 3.6.103 (Conflated Text). This and all future Shakespeare references are to *The Norton Shakespeare, Based on the Oxford Edition,* ed. Stephen Greenblatt et al. (New York: Norton, 1997).

It is not possible to know when or how often nouns functioned as verbs in my early life, but babies might be as adept in their manipulation of grammatical function as they are in touching their toes while lying on their back.

HURRICANE

There is a blank page in an early handwritten draft of this book. On Sunday, August 28, 2011, Hurricane Irene sweeps up the East Coast. For the first time in its history, New York City is on lockdown: buses, subways, trains, airplanes taken out of service; major highways shut down; thousands forced to evacuate homes in low-lying areas; hospital patients in the city moved to other facilities. In coastal Connecticut, precautions are taken: highways are closed, trains cancelled. If you refuse to evacuate houses near the water, you sign a waiver and list next of kin. The evening news shows a startling image of New York's Grand Central Station completely empty.

Between 10 a.m. and 11 a.m., Hurricane Irene severs enormous limbs from an ancient linden tree in the front courtyard of our apartment building. People walk by, pause, gape, take photographs with cell phones; neighbors stand transfixed in mourning; children dance about the unaccustomed nearness of huge fallen branches. The day before, David and I loaded up the bathtub and every large container in the apartment with water; made six days of coffee, three days of tea, and eight trays of ice; wrapped important papers and our writing in dry cleaning bags; collected candles and flashlights; moved sentimental objects from windows to closets; put wallets and money and car registration in the one tiny hall without windows. We listened to the sound of wind roaring in the chimney while shadows of treetops flickered across the window panes.

By mid-afternoon the sun is out; the wind has become a healthy breeze amid post-storm heat and humidity. Cars and pedestrians pass by. We are lucky. Over five million people lost electricity with an estimated seven billion dollars of damage on the Eastern seaboard. I see the heart-shaped leaves of the fallen linden branches shake in the left-over wind.

There is no "hurricane," not even "wind," in my 200-word list. How would I have named this event? "Wawa!"

One week after Hurricane Irene, the sun is shining. There are still twice-a-day robo calls from the mayor reporting the lessening number of homes and buildings without power or water, along with specifications for curbside removal of trees and debris. Lighthouse Point Beach reopens to visitors, as if summer is getting a second chance.

David sits under the shade of our beach umbrella, reading; I recklessly soak up the sun. Post-hurricane signs read: "No swimming." I ask about wading. No wading. A handful of people in bathing suits dot the beach. Near our umbrella a young mother talks to her daughter: "[No more] spitting"; "Sit"; "Water"; "Ready to go bye-bye?"; "Come on, baby." The tiny girl, clutching her water bottle, never speaks. I could not have been that child.

In our sun-soaked living room, I check the 200-word list: "no more," "sit down," water ("wawa"), "come," "baby," "bye-bye." There is "shade"—-but no "sun."

I try to imagine a world with no sun. I cannot. But, of course, I must. I lived there long ago.

NOT ON THE LIST

There are certain letters of the alphabet for which no words are listed, for example, *v*. Roberta Golinkoff and Kathy Hirsh-Pasek explain that "sounds. . .produced during the first two years roughly correspond to the letter sounds *p, m, h, n, w,* and *b*. Sounds like *r* and *l* don't generally sound adult-like until children are between the ages of 3 and 6. Sounds like *k, g,* and *t* don't emerge until between ages 2 and 4. *F* and *y* first appear between 2.5 years and 4 years and *ch, sh, z, j,* and *v* come in somewhere between 3.5 years and 8 years. Not until 8 are all of these sounds fully formed in a vocal cavity that resembles that of the adult."[85]

Now I imagine a 200-word world without *v*: without "victim," "victory," "vice," "vice-president," "vines," "vanity," "virgin," "vacation," "vacuity," "vagina," "valentine," "valedictorian," or "vang" (a word I've never used: a rope running from the peak of a gaff to a ship's rail or mast, used to steady the gaff).

I am now in the position of a child for whom almost every new sound has to be deciphered. Gaff, I learn, is a spar attached to the mast and used to extend the upper edge of a fore-and-aft sail. A spar is a wooden or metal pole, such as a mast, boom, yard, or bowsprit, used to support sails and rigging. A bowsprit, I discover, is a spar, extending forward from the prow of a ship, to which the stays of the foremast are fashioned, while a boom is apparently a spar extending from a mast to hold or extend the foot of a sail. A yard is not what I had thought at all but a long tapering spar slung to a mast to support and spread the head of a square sail, lugsail, or lateen.[86] Eventually I will look up the meanings of lugsail and lateen.

"Spar" and "boom" and "yard," unentangled from their nautical context, are accessible, easy to learn and use, yet construed quite differently when called up by "vang." As enticing new words enter a child's vocabulary, the puzzle of identical sounds with different meanings eventually makes an appearance (for example, "vein" and "vain").

Other "v" words now come to mind: "vanish," "varicose," "Velcro," "vent," "vertigo," "veto," "Viagra," "vicissitude," "violence."

---

85. Golinkoff and Hirsh-Pasek, 138. Erika Hoff notes that while *v* "is a relatively late-appearing sound" among "children acquiring English,. . .children can get fairly far making different words sound different without mastering *v*." Hoff, 167-168.

86. *American Heritage Dictionary*, 1515, 565, 1327, 171, 165, 1587.

These "v" words invite stories almost every adult knows and can tell. My 200-word world is limited but also enhanced by what is not yet there.

SHADOWS AND OUTLINES

I learn from a friend who is a physician that the eye begins to develop early in pregnancy. She writes: "The fact that the eye can constrict or dilate during fetal development does not tell me if there is any light in the womb to detect. [When] babies are born prematurely,. . . we can see that a baby's pupil constricts and dilates. I would think that there is normally no light in the womb. I have to look into this further."

I receive further information:

> . . .if there were a source of light or some detectable light inside the womb, the fetal eye might perceive it as the eye seems to be open at times. It would seem that the best the fetal eye could do would be to perceive objects in its view, but not at all clearly. So maybe [it would be] like sitting in a very dark room without your glasses on. If the room has any light at all, your pupil eventually dilates enough that you can see outlines or objects not clearly. Maybe the fetus sees this? There must be so little light that I can't imagine the fetal eye could see much more than shadows and outlines.[87]

The "fetal eye" prepares us for language, with its own shadowy outlines in infanthood.

---

87. Dr. Lynn Montz, email correspondence, September 10 and September 13, 2011.

ART OF ANOTHER KIND

David and I visit "Art of Another Kind," an exhibit at the Guggenheim Museum. On a placard describing Giuseppe Capogrossi's painting, "Surface 210 [Superficie 210]," I read: "in 1949, [Capogrossi] developed a vocabulary of irregular comb- or fork-shaped signs. With no allegorical, psychological, or symbolic meaning, these structural elements could be assembled and connected in countless variations. Intricate and insistent, Capogrossi's signs determined the construction of the pictorial surface. Similar to mysterious lists or sequences, his paintings were immediate in their appeal yet remained hard to decode."

A baby's jabbering—insistent, possibly intricate, certainly hard to decode—contains structural elements that might be assembled and connected in countless variations.

The entrance into language is art of another kind.

CIRCLING THE LIST

I circle the list. It's an enigma. How was it created? Certainly my parents never heard all these words spoken in a single day. Did they make other lists, with other words, now lost? The 200 recorded words come forward to meet me, revive forgotten episodes, raise unanswered questions. I try to get behind these words before they found a home in my life.

Suppose that the first words listed beneath each letter of the alphabet were the first words my parents heard their child speak: apple, birdie, clock (tick tock), door, eyes, fruit, grass, here it is, jello, kitty, light, man, nice, otto (!), piece, rock (repeated), socks, train (choo choo), ulain, what's this, yes.

Not too bad. Of course, there is no mama and daddy, no book or baby, no good girl, no kiss or milk or outside, no Susan—not even a "Hi there." But it is a world of some interest.

A book I am reading by Natalie Goldberg asks: "Exactly how do you feel about apples?"[88] How did I feel about apples? I love them now and cut them with a small knife as I watched my paternal grandfather do, peeling off the skin in one long stroke and then separating the shining exposed fruit into four sections, seeds removed. My first "apple" must have been far different: applesauce eaten with a little spoon or placed inside my mouth by careful hands. Was "apple" a command or an acknowledgment—or perhaps a refusal, announced with a head shake? Exactly how *did* I feel about apples? A simple question with no simple answer, with no answers at all.

And yet there it is: the first word in the list—only because it begins with the first letter of the alphabet. I make a doubtful entry into a world entered through a list of words.

I try "birdie." A friend named Birdie lived across the street from our house when I was about twelve years old. What kinds of birdies did I see or like long before that? My mother would have pointed out any birds nearby. What was my first experience of birdness? Exactly how did I feel about that?

But then maybe "birdie" was just one of the sounds I loved to hear, sounds like those I may have heard in the womb uttered by loving voices.

---

88. Natalie Goldberg, *Old Friend from Far Away* (New York: Free Press, 2007), 137.

THE JOB OF THE BABY

"The job of the baby is to learn," Dr. Elizabeth Spelke tells us. She adds: "What's special about language is its productive combinatorial power. . . . We can use it to combine anything with anything."[89] Tonight in a neighborhood restaurant, a baby at a nearby table emits shrill sounds at regular intervals, producing nothing more than parental embarrassment. I hear "naw" and "wah," repeated several times between oases of silence. I wonder what those sounds mean to her. They don't seem to be either a command or an indication of any particular need beyond that of expression itself.

I sort through the list my parents made: 104 one-syllable words; 47 two-syllable words; one three-syllable word (banana); 22 phrases of "combinatorial power," some quite interesting; and nine representations of sounds associated with words not otherwise listed (e.g., tick tock, bow wow). Rhymes are mainly repetitions or near repetitions (moo moo, kack-kack, choo choo, ding dong).

I have a particular soundscape. I say "walk," "wall," and "wash," but "wawa" instead of "water." I say "there it is," but "ta ta" instead of "thank you." Children "differ in the particular sounds they produce," Erika Hoff points out. "These differences may be due to differences in articulatory ability, but some children just seem to like certain sounds."[90] How elegantly simple this explanation is, and how welcome. Some children just seem to like certain sounds.

Rhymes and onomatopoeia might be my first language. My baby self produces self-pleasing sounds, voicings not yet language. I am lost in imagining a world like that.

I seem to love two-syllable words that end with a strong stress on the same sound, *e*: "auntie," "baby," "birdie," "daddy," "Danny," "dirty," "hanky," "kitty," "money," "pussy," "penny," "rosy," "Ricky," "toidy," "trolley," "tummy." I also seem to collect words with the same initial

---

89. Dr. Elizabeth S. Spelke, quoted by Natalie Angier, "Profiles in Science/ Elizabeth S. Spelke: From the Minds of Babies," *New York Times*, May 1, 2012, D4.
90. Hoff, 169. Hoff also notes that "in English, the initial sound in *the* and *this* very frequently heard because it is used in a few very high-frequency words. However, because that sound is not involved in many different words, its functional significance is low, and it is acquired late in children acquiring English."

letter. Twenty-five words begin with *b*, eighteen words with *t*;[91] *c* and *s* tie for third place with fifteen words apiece;[92] *j* and *y* have one word each; *i*, *q*, *v*, *x*, and *z* have none.

The makers of the list are listening for words, not sounds. In very early babyhood there is no actual "learning" of words. The list registers sounds I liked, remembered, experienced—sounds that would eventually become "words." The baby's first job is a matter of sound, as it was when she spilt forth into light and breath.

---

91. I do not count "train" as a *t* word because it is entered as "choo choo," but then add "tick tock" from the list of *c* words.

92. The number of *c* words is limited to fifteen because I remove "clock," entered as "tick tock," and also "cow," represented by "moo moo."

A BABY'S BUSINESS

Two women walk slowly behind a group of small children. One of them says to a little boy not too far ahead of her:

Jeffrey, don't do that.

After a muffled comment by Jeffrey, I hear her response:

It's none of your business.

I doubt, perhaps a little naively, if as a child I ever heard those words. In my early language-learning life, everything would have been my business.

DREAMING

A young Mexican boy, forced to relocate to his family's native land after his father is deported, says: "I dream, like, I'm sleeping in the United States. But when I wake up, I'm in Mexico."[93]

When I dreamed as a baby, did I dream in images that had no words, like my dog Cocoa when she twitched, probably chasing squirrels in her sleep? Oliver Sacks asserts, startlingly, that congenitally blind people who have never had any visual experience "sometimes report having clear and recognizable visual elements in their dreams." He mentions that "blind subjects were able, upon waking, to draw the visual components of their dreams." In my near-blind state inside the womb, was there visual activity with no recourse to recording it by voice or hand? Sacks adds that "there is increasing evidence for the extraordinarily rich interconnectedness and interactions of the sensory areas of the brain, and the difficulty, therefore, of saying that anything is purely visual or purely auditory, or purely anything."[94]

When did my small world of words enter my dreams?

Could I dream a word before I uttered it? "We are such stuff/ As dreams are made on, and our little life/ Is rounded with a sleep," Shakespeare's Prospero says.[95] Was my slowly growing world of 200 words the stuff of my dreams, or was there another whole dream life, a lost language gradually replaced by the words I came to know and never dreamt again once I learned the words I learned?[96]

Suppose each word I dreamt into utterance told a story. Suppose each word tells a story of the stuff dreams are made on.

---

93. Damien Cave, "American Children, Now Struggling to Adjust to Life in Mexico," *New York Times*, June 19, 2012, A3.
94. Oliver Sacks, *The Mind's Eye*, 237n17, 237-38.
95. Shakespeare, *The Tempest*: 4.1.156-158.
96. "Sllt. Almost human the way it sllt to call attention. Doing its level best to speak. That door too sllt creaking, asking to be shut. Everything speaks in its own way. Sllt." James Joyce, *Ulysses* (New York: Random House, 1946), 120.

GIVEN AND FOUND

If there is a list, there were listeners, responding, interacting, remembering, recording. When did all this listening take place? Were there morning words and evening words? Were some words first reported by someone else?

On a late evening television show, *Chelsea Lately*, several male comedians sit, a few days after Father's Day, with their young sons on their laps. One very young boy begins speaking immediately, throwing off the adults' comic timing at every turn. At one point, Chelsea Handler says, loudly: "Benjamin, shut up!" Benjamin persists and after futile attempts by his father to quiet him (hand over mouth, offers of cereal and bits of fruit, whispers of "quiet"), the baby's "talk" becomes a part of the talk show.

Finally, Chelsea interrupts the comedian who is trying to speak during the little boy's constant chatter: "Let him talk. He obviously ha a lot to say." Except for a few words ("Daddy's show"), what Benjamin has to say is unintelligible. And yet he does not stop talking until confronted with a direct question. "Do you think I'm beautiful?" Chelsea asks with a laugh in her voice. Silence. His world of language has no bridge to hers.[97]

When did my "talk" became sufficiently intelligible? Did I produce parts—beginnings, middles, or ends—of words corrected and completed by a parent? When something was named over and over, how long did it take to connect sound and object? When did I learn to initiate this process myself, asking, "What's this?" and "What's that?" Perhaps "What's this?" and "What's that?" were imitations of my parents' voices before I even understood that I was asking questions or what it was I was asking. "What's this?" and "What's that?" would have been a full-time job.

I wonder now what I wanted most: to "talk"; to be heard; to be responded to with new or familiar sounds; or simply to join, be part of, world of sounds.

Once I "knew" a word, used it more than once, directed it confidentl at my toes or someone's nose or a nearby tree, it would be *my* language not the language of the one who had offered it to me. As a particular sound became a familiar presence, it was becoming a new kind of companion—and a link to. . .to what?

---

97. *Chelsea Lately*, E! Network, June 19, 2012, 12:30 a.m.

Before "apple" linked itself to an apple, did it circle back as simply one more sound, my own, my new way of being present in a world filled with sounds I had never heard before? My self-delighting job as a baby was a continual discovery of voicing.

* * *

I don't think conversations in my tiny world of 200 words could have been very interesting, but I'm sure my mother, a former teacher, would have engaged in them with some pleasure.

Here is a possible version of one of our "conversations":

"Look at the birdie."
"Yes, that's a *birdie*."
"Another *birdie*" (different bird).
"*Bye-bye, birdie*."

"Look at your *toes*."
"Yes, they are your *toes*."
"Can we count them? One, *two, three. . . .*"

"See the *birdie* [new bird] on that *tree*?"
"*Hi there, birdie*."

"*Daddy* is home."
"Time for *bed*."

"No, those are *mama's glasses*."
"*Night night*."

"Where is the *kitty* now?"
"Don't pull *kitty's tail*."

"This is *mama's hat*."

"Where is your *doll?*"
"*Here it is*."
"*Good girl*."

Boring. But not then.

My earliest speech would not have been constructed grammatically, like the talk above. Words, as Kathryn Hirsh-Pasek and Roberta Golinkoff observe, "connect to the world in very different ways"; concrete "nouns do so more transparently than verbs."[98]

I imagine my words strung together without verbs:

"Daddy bus."
"Daddy hat."
"dress dirty."
"music, more."
"bear mine."
"ti ti done."
"kitty nice."
"outside dark" [Did I ever say "dark outside"?].

Where are my verbs? I count possibly 29: build, back (put back), come, close (door), clean (probably an adjective), draw, fall down, here it is, dance (possibly a noun), kiss (same possibility), more (an adverb used as a verb?), night night (possibly a verb), push, pat, read, scratch, sit down, swing (no doubt a noun), scrub, spank, squeeze, there it is, that's all, tip toe, walk, wash, up (adverb used as a verb), and my all-time favorites—what's this?, what's that? (Also, but doubtful, are: hop, hop; rock, rock; "row, row"; "ring a round a rosy.")

About one-seventh of my 200 words are verbs. For an infant, pointing is the verb. One of my jobs as a baby was learning about things, beings, I could see, hear, eat, touch. With my nouns, I could express the existence of what lay in my path, came to meet me, was arranged before or beneath or around me, flew over my head, caressed and bathed and fed and spoke to me. The actions and occurrences of my babyhood appear to be mainly small, domestic, house-bound, but still there is a desire to go beyond what is given to me to know: *what's this?, what's that?*

As Daniel Stern writes in *Diary of a Baby,* "The word is, at the same time, given and found."[99]

---

98. Kathryn A. Hirsh-Pasek and Roberta M. Golinkoff, eds., *Action Meets Verb: How Children Learn Verbs* (Oxford: Oxford University Press, 2006), 544. http:/www.oxfordscholarship.com/view/10.1093/acprof:oso/97801. Accessed January 30, 2013.
99. Stern, 111.

HAPPY BIRTHDAY ACROSS THE OCEAN

On June 25 I telephone my best friend from college, now living in Oxford, to wish her a happy birthday. Sue's three grandchildren have brought her a dead snake as a present. She takes her mobile phone upstairs along with Sasha, her youngest grandchild, not yet three, where they are to have a tea party with eleven stuffed animals. As we continue to talk, I hear Sue say to Sasha: "I didn't know you knew the word 'disgusting.'"

At first, Sasha is reluctant to talk to me on the phone but, when encouraged by her grandmother to sing, she manages the first two lines of "Happy Birthday," and then begins a song about a spider. Soon comes a torrent of sound. Sasha is on a roll. While I can only make out a few words here and there, she loves "talking" to me. When her grandmother is able to regain control of her phone, she tells me that Sasha tried to give me a piece of pink candy and then attempted to show me a photo of Sue and her late husband, Colin Matthew.

Sasha's flood of "talk" is mainly a one-way conversation, much like the first sounds a baby hears. Her sweet offer of food via a trans-Atlantic call, like her showing the phone a picture, would be an imitation of parents who "give" and "show." But the talking comes first.

Talk, give, show. Talking that picks up song and unexpected "adult" words like "disgusting" is the child's gift and show.

Sue's birthday present isn't just a dead snake and a tea party. Sasha is presenting her voice, even her new word, to her granny. I could hear that from across the ocean.

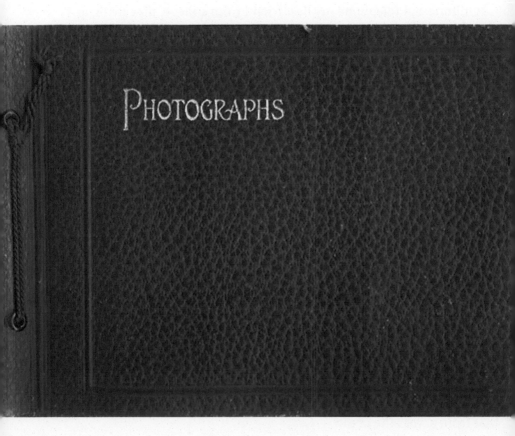

THE ALBUM

D. W. Winnicott has said, "There is no such thing as a baby. . . . [I]f you set out to describe a baby, you will find you are describing a baby and someone."[100]

The album of baby pictures is brown leather, worn, with braided brown yarn strung through two holes in the front and back covers. The white letters on its faded front cover say simply, "Photographs." On its first rectangular black page is written, in white ink, the words, "SUSAN BARBARA LETZLER," underscored by a wavy line that circles down at one end and up at the other. This is the same handwriting that captions each black-and-white snapshot, usually three to a page. Each image is held in place by four old-fashioned, wedge-shaped photo mounting corners. Much care has gone into this visual record of my infanthood in a non-digital era. I give much care to it now as I look for possible clues to the contexts and creation of my 200-word vocabulary.

Four weeks old, I sit in the lap of my young mother, her right hand over my right shoulder, fingers curled. Her left hand holds my hand as she gazes at the photographer, probably my father, probably at his request. A second snapshot shows her gazing down at her baby dressed in a long, flowing white gown.

100. Quoted by Andrew Solomon, "YOU WILL KNOW THEM *by* THE LIGHT IN THEIR EYES", in Edward Mapplethorpe, *One: Sons of Daughters* (Brooklyn: powerhouse Books, 2016), n.p.

DOLL BABY

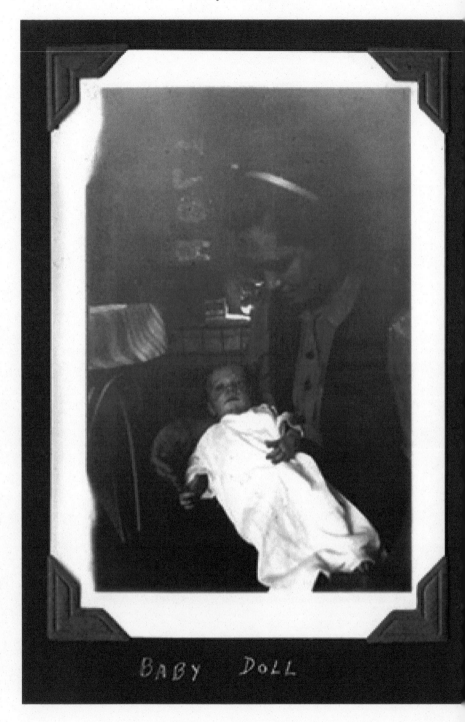

BABY DOLL

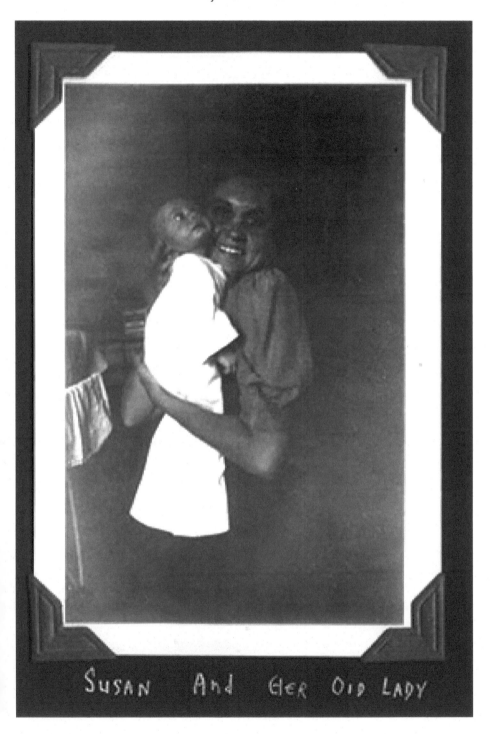

The first image is captioned "Doll Baby"; the second is captioned "Baby Doll." In this playful reversal of two words, what interests me now, as i would have then, is the different sounds of these two phrases.

In my first few weeks of life I probably heard these words again and again in my mother's soothing voice. I would have come to love the sounds of "baby" and "doll," "doll" and "baby," because of their voicing when she was near, without attaching a particular meaning or association with myself.

"Baby doll," "doll baby." I say them over to myself, aloud, not knowing where my mother put the stresses. I say them many different ways, trying to reproduce (impossible) her voice. It is hypnotic. I can almost feel them enter my body, lulling me and bringing me awake at the same time. I forget the meanings I know. The two phrases, repeated, become more and more distinct. "Doll" lengthens in "baby doll" and shortens in "doll baby," an effect reversed with "baby."

I hear these sounds as one- or two-syllable words, units with discrete and different beats. My four-week-old self would have heard "baby doll" or "doll baby" as one long sound. Erika Hoff notes that the "first problem for the child is how to find the word within the stream of speech."[101] "Hi there," "fall down," "good girl," "that's all"—along with the three-word phrases, "there it is" and "here it is"—were, like "daddy" and "doctor," first a string of sounds that produced an effect on the listener, a stream of speech that gave pleasure.

The caption is a voice looking at a picture. I have entered the photograph as if my mother were actually speaking, or had been speaking, or were about to speak, words to a four-week-old baby who was perhaps listening and perhaps remembering. Through its caption, the still image has taken life.

In another snapshot, I am in the same white flowing gown, held cheek-to-cheek as my mother smiles at the camera. My head, carefully cradled by her fingers, tilts upward in an open-eyed gaze. The snapshot of my twenty-eight-year-old mother beaming at her four-week-old baby is captioned, "Susan and her old lady." The caption no longer identifies me as a "baby" or a "doll" but as a *Susan*.

I say my name over and over. Each time, it sounds different—literally—because I am self-conscious, as if it is a word newly arrived, as it once was: "Susan, Susan." I hear it not in my usual voice, as if

---

101. "How do...[children] distinguish word boundaries?" The child must find "word boundaries" in others' speech. One clue is "recognizing recurring sound sequences" in words heard over and over; "[s]tress, or rhythm, is one other clue." Hoff, 204-205.

introducing myself to students in my class or guests at a party, but spoken by the woman who with my father gave me that name and perhaps savors it as it registers the changing nature of the child who will ultimately recognize it as her own.

"Susan" does not have the same effect when repeated as "doll" and "baby." It seems to take more effort to get straight through—more air flow, ending in a kind of growl which I never noticed before. Hoff confirms that "word learning begins months before children speak their first words. Children as young as 5 months selectively respond to certain words . . . . The first word children seem to respond to is their own name." Golinkoff and Hirsh-Pasek add an important qualification:

> researchers were stunned to learn that babies
> preferred to hear their own names over names with
> identical [syllable] stress. Does this mean that
> babies *know* that they are hearing their own names?
> Do they understand that this is what *they* are called?
> Experts think this is doubtful. It is more likely
> that before babies know their own name, they recognize
> the sounds that compose their name. . .. But no one
> really knows when babies first have this realization
> [that] their names refer to them.[102]

"Susan" may have been heard early and often. The concept of self-as-Susan would come later.

In another snapshot, the caption "What's up?" gives voice to a diapered baby lying prone in a crib, feet raised jauntily. My mouth is open, as if in speech. I gaze with what seems to be concentrated interest at something just outside the left edge of the photograph. I seem to be asking, in a private unrecorded language, my own version of "What's up?"

On the following page, two adjoining snapshots are captioned "Uh, uh. Don't cry!" and "Shhhh!" "Uh, uh. Don't cry!" is addressed to a diapered baby whose expressive fingers and slightly dispirited look signal distress threatening to become vocal. "Shhhh" captions an image of the same diapered baby lying in her crib with eyes closed and mouth partly open. The caption is the voice of a parent concerned that her child sleep peacefully and undisturbed.

---

102. Hoff, 195. Golinkoff and Hirsh-Pasek, 53. At the age of one year, my brother's version of "Susan" was "Su Sa." Was this my own early version of my name—and when did I add the *n*?

I imagine my lips resisting a cry that has no word for itself.

A later page headed "Summer School" presents three snapshots, captioned in this informative sequence: "Pretty Young To Be Reading"; "It's Really Not a Book"; "It's a Rattle." In the first image, my two-month-old self lies on a small blanket outdoors, head raised, eyes focused on what looks very much like the pages of a book. The last image, in clearer focus, identifies the object of my intense gaze as a rattle.

This sequence of snapshots shows my interest in a toy that produces a succession of repeated sounds, mimicking the noise I come to know a words. This is what I am learning in "summer school."

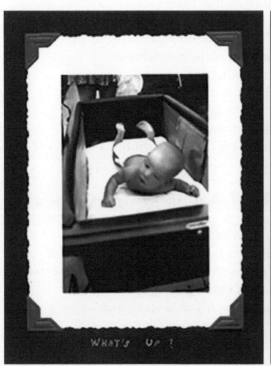

WHAT'S UP ?

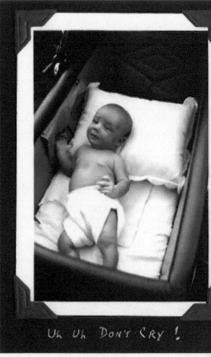

Uh Uh DON'T CRY !

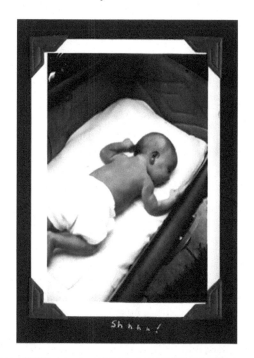

Shhhh!

SUMMER SCHOOL

YOUNG TO BE READING

IT'S REALLY NOT A BOOK . . . . .

IT'S A RATTLE.

8 OLD   5-5-40

VENTRILOQUIZED

Another snapshot in the photo album shows a smiling young mother, in three-quarters profile, the fingers of her right hand outstretched, just barely touching the bottom of a glass of orange juice her seven-month-old daughter is drinking. I am in a baby chair with a circular tray attached by straps that reach back toward its well-padded side. The focus of the photograph is on the baby whose eyes are turned toward the camera. The caption reads: "Don't help me!"

The voice is that of a baby admonishing her mother. I look at the baby looking back at me. She does not know the language in the caption, but her confident outward gaze seems to speak those words.

A second snapshot on this page shows me holding the glass independently. My mother is barely visible, her hands clasped near her own body, at a distance from her child. The baby again gazes at the camera, further marginalizing the mother. The caption reads: "I can hold it alone!" A seven-month-old parades her independence and her expertise in downing a glass of orange juice. Visually she seems to be saying, "I can hold it alone."

At eight months, I am pictured outdoors, in my carriage, in winter. I wear a knitted, white wool hat with two tassels, a long-sleeved white jacket, and white mittens. I am cradling a small doll who is also wearing a white cap. Quite content, I smile at someone outside the left frame of the picture. The caption reads: "A Nice Day in Winter." Directly beneath is a second photo, taken from a different angle. We see the other side of the hooded carriage out of which I am peering, straining as if to see someone who ought to be visible but isn't. My expression is quizzical, bordering on distress. The independence of the orange juice drinking has disappeared. The caption reads: "Where *did* they go?"

In the center of a large, flowered sofa, I sit on my mother's lap, a tiny right hand pressed against her chest, sock-clad feet dangling over her thigh. She gazes downward at her baby who looks elsewhere with great interest, searching the space just outside the left frame of the photograph. The caption reads: "Where's Daddy?" In a second image on the same page of the album, the smiling baby's gaze is directed just beyond the *right* frame of the photograph. The caption reads: "There he is!" But where *is* Daddy? I have no one to ask about these small mysteries. The caption gives voice to a baby's shifting gaze, from left to right, as she finds her father.

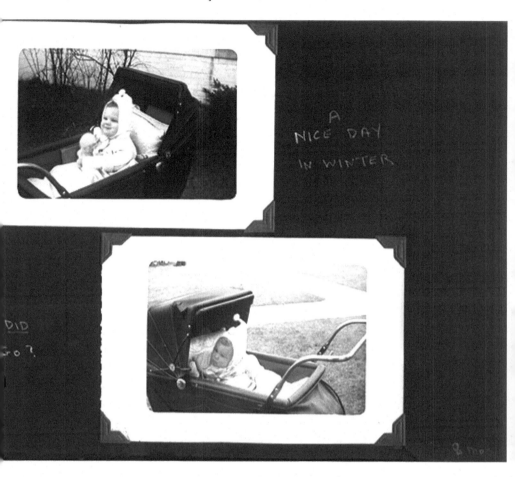

A
NICE DAY
IN WINTER

DID

o ?

Ventriloquized "talking" in the photo album takes place in "the space between what can be seen and what can be spoken."[103]

I come upon a dialogue, in slow motion, between mother and daughter, presented in a sequence of three images. In the first, my mother tries to spoon-feed her nine-month-old baby whose lips remain resolutely closed. The caption reads: "Ma: `Time to eat.'" In the second image, my mother opens her own mouth in demonstration as she offers food to a more receptive daughter: "Ma: `See, like this.'" In the third image, she holds a bowl into which my fingers have traveled. The caption reads: "Susan: `I like it *this* way.'"

This is the only captioned dialogue in the photo album. I hear my mother saying these words, "Time to eat," in her own voice, so hard to recover but suddenly present. I imagine her adding, "See, like this," and myself perhaps resisting. I don't hear myself declare, with supreme confidence, "I like it *this* way," but when I look again at the image, that is what I seem to be saying.

Marilyn May Vihman states that

> silent gestures are reported to occur, at least in some infants, as probable precursors to vocal production. . ... Such non-verbal "practice" or exercise of the articulatory gesture involved in vocalization, but without phonation [speech sounds] and thus with no auditory effect, strongly suggests attention to the visual effects produced by talking faces. . ..
>
> The critical importance of the caretaker's face has been emphasized by psychologists interested in newborns. . ..[I]t is proprioception [the unconscious perception of movement and spatial orientation that arises from stimuli within the body]. . .which can be said to drive surprisingly precocious reproduction of adult behavior.

---

103. Lyana Lynn Haupt, *Pilgrim on the Great Bird Continent: The Importance of Everything and Other Lessons from Darwin's Lost Notebooks* (New York: Little, Brown and Company, 2006), 257.

LUNCH TIME

A:-"TIME TO EAT"

MA:-"SEE, LIKE THIS"

SUSAN:-"I LIKE IT T

She adds: "The sight of a speaker's lips moving silently as in speech may evoke a vocal response from the child."[104]

Almost at the end of the album, I suddenly find an actual image of voicing. I am ten-and-a-half months old, seated in a stroller, hugging my bunny. In an adjoining photo, I stand up, leaning on the handle of the stroller, bunny nowhere in sight. The caption reads: "A Speech." My mouth is open, not in surprise or dismay but in utterance. Now I am no longer looking at words. I am listening to a photograph of me talking.

---

104. Marilyn May Vihman, *Phonological Development: The Origins of Language in the Child* (Cambridge: Blackwell, 1996), 120, 121n.

BOREDOM

Adam Gopnik suggests that "having your picture taken is a strange circumstance, deserving of some extended mental scrutiny."[105] Edward Mapplethorpe's collection of photographs of unnamed, one-year-old babies shows faces that are quizzical, wary, sulky, smiling broadly with a few new teeth on display, fearful, pensive, skeptical, shy, anxious, perplexed, self-delighted, and distressed to the point of tears, but I doubt that any of them are bored. As Dr. Samantha Boardman says, "Babies are born curious." By the age of one, "these little beings [are] on the brink of personhood, bursting with energy and insatiable craving to discover the world around them."[106] Unlike the rest of us, how could they be bored?

There are general theories of why attention wanes (or ceases at all, which for practical purposes I am calling "boredom"): either the task at hand is not interesting or it demands attentional abilities we adults are not inclined to provide. Monica Rosenberg has attempted to identify a way to measure adult attention based on a person's "unique pattern of brain connectivity."[107] She suggests that "infants pay special attention to novel events, which helps them maximize the amount of new information that they learn from the world."[108] For infants so many experiences could be novel events, beginning with their unmediated cry at birth.

My guess is that the attentional resources required when a camera is pointed at one are not depleted in the baby my father lovingly photographed.

---

105. Adam Gopnik, "Baby Face." Quoted in Mapplethorpe, n.p. Gopnik adds: "The child is a theory tester, a knowledge collector." Ibid.
106. Quoted in Mapplethorpe, n.p.
107. Monica Rosenberg, "Brain connections predict how well you can pay attention," *The Conversation* (2015). https://theconversation.com/brain-connections-predict-how-well-you-can-pay-attention-51082. Accessed July 9, 2016.
108. Monica Rosenberg, email correspondence, July 12, 2016.

TWENTY-TWO WORDS

Twenty-two words in the list of my 200-word vocabulary at the age of eighteen months also appear in the captions of the photo album. What can that tell me? "Although differences in language-learning opportunities account for a great deal of the individual differences in vocabulary size, children also contribute to the process," Erika Hoff writes. "It takes two to achieve the mutual engagement that benefits language-advancing."[109] Both the list and the album of baby pictures represent the interactions and the interests of parent and child.

Imitation is a primary mode of language acquisition for a baby. Among these twenty-two words might be my first word.

Baby
Doll   [also doll referring to a toy, not a baby]
Susan
Up
Cry[ing]
Birdie
Read
Book
Grandpa [papa]
Bath
Chair
Up [repeated]
Orange juice
Tip Toe
Daddy
There [he] is [list: there it is]
Grandma [list: gmama]
Ball
Carriage
Orange
Tooth [list: teeth]
Shoes

---

109. Hoff, 202.

My attempt to find a significant correspondence, or any correspondence at all, between a written record of the words spoken in the first eighteen months of a baby's life and captioned visual images of that baby from the age of four weeks to eleven months has many problems. The two time periods don't coincide. The captioned words may not have been spoken to, or heard by, the baby when the photograph was taken. The list of 200 words may not be complete and the sub-listings under each letter of the alphabet may represent not the order in which each new word was mastered (though, in some cases, they might), but the order in which the words were remembered by the list-makers. There is no indication of which words under *A* may have preceded, or followed, words under *C* or *D* or *P*.

And yet.

The author of the captions is the co-author of the list: a listener and recorder, a witness and speaker/ventriloquist. My mother's love of words, evident in the keeping and preserving of the list, as well as in the captions that accompany the visual record of her child's early life, would have passed on to her daughter, to me in my babyhood.

The language of the captions might represent language I heard and repeated. In these twenty-two words there is possibly a clue, attenuated and undiscovered, to my first utterance.

PART 3: KNOWING AND NOT KNOWING

SPACELAB

For 24 hours I have been wearing a black Spacelab battery holder with a strap that hangs over my right shoulder. It is attached by a red wire to a blue Spacelab blood pressure monitor that makes a soft whirring sound every 20-30 minutes, followed by a series of clicks. As the cuff around my left arm tightens, the pressure cuts off my blood flow; when the pressure is released, blood starts flowing again. The monitor will take measurements to see if my heart is working too hard.

In her 70s, my mother was also told she had elevated blood pressure, but no one gave her a 24-hour monitor (she was already a cancer patient), only a recommendation to cut down on salt and the pickled herring which no one else in our family ever ate.

A languageless appendage is intimately related to my heart, my blood. It communicates so often that it has become my friend.

Was that true of us, when I softly whirred and sent an inarticulate message to my mother as her blood coursed through, giving me life before I was born?

PATTERNS AND CONNECTIONS

In *The Boy Detective: A New York Childhood*, Roger Rosenblatt tells a story about his grandfather who listens as he turns an account of his day into a creative fantasy about an alligator with gold and silver teeth and a friendly black bear whose cave contains cones of cotton candy. In seeing his grandfather's "look of amused attentiveness," the young boy "also saw the power of words."

I was a youthful teller of tales and I too must have felt the effects of the attention paid to such efforts. Perhaps even in my baby babble and tentative use of language, I received looks of amused attentiveness. It is very tempting to find links between one's early relation to language and one's adult vocation as writer. But Rosenblatt offers caution: "I tell the story of my grandfather as if he urged me on my way. But I don't think it's so. . .. More likely. . ..It is one of those memories we find to create patterns and connections in our lives where none exist."[110]

To say now what I could or could not say while my early vocabulary was being recorded is as problematic as the seeking of patterns and connections where perhaps none exist.

---

110. Roger Rosenblatt, *The Boy Detective: A New York Childhood* (New York: HarperCollins, 2013), 88, 90.

TECHNOLOGY

In graduate school, a man I had been seeing told me that when he was a child he didn't speak for the first several years of his life. Then one day, on the second floor of his Cambridge house, he suddenly announced: "Coming down the stairs is me." Quite remarkable. But I doubt that he was the one who first remembered this. As with photographs of our childhood, we take our recollections from what others have witnessed and preserved—or not. Without my parents' visual and written records, I would have no way to recover the language of my infant world.

Today, of course, there are abundant and ever-increasing technological means for recording almost every instant of our life, before and after birth. Somini Sengupta reports on an online service that helps parents "keep tabs on every chat, post, and photo that floats across their children's Facebook pages." A survey by the Pew Research Center found that nearly 40 percent of parents followed their children on Facebook and Twitter, a monitoring that often led to family arguments. One father used a text message application called textPlus that allowed him "to be copied on every text message his teenage son sends his girlfriend." Technology "is at least as nimble as adolescents, and neither parents nor the technology they buy can always read a teenager's mind." As for pre-teens, a "version of Apple's mobile operating system offered a single-app mode so a parent can lock a toddler into one activity on an iPad." Lock a toddler into one activity on an iPad? Technology monitors "children's footprints" so that parents can have conversations about electronic conversation they have accessed electronically.[111]

Apparently, it is possible to "rig your household with technology to measure and filter how your children use technology, from potty training to prom"[112]—technology monitoring technology. If I had been born now, there might be a complete electronic record of sounds, words, images. I might know the first message I ever received or posted. I might construct my own alphabetized lists and carefully organized, photoshopped pictures of myself and my activities.

---

111. Somini Sengupta, "'Big Brother'? No, It's Parents," *New York Times*, June 26 2012, B4.
112. Somini Sengupta, "Tools to Control a Child's Technology," *New York Times* June 26, 2012, B4.

And what would I know then about my relationship to language and its sounds? Certainly these technological innovations represent an ever-greater need for expressivity, as well as a greater involvement in its surveillance.

But I remain transfixed by a handwritten list of 200 words and captions accompanying black-and-white snapshots of a baby finding her way to the power, and pleasure, of speech.

INSOMNIA

The nineteenth-century British poet Alfred Lord Tennyson writes:

So runs my dream; but what am I?
  An infant crying in the night;
  An infant crying for the light,
And with no language but a cry.[113]

In a TV commercial, a husband and wife in bed at night hear their baby cry in the next room. The husband responds by taking his young son for a ride in his car, driving around and around a circular driveway in front of the house. We see the baby looking up at a full moon from the back seat, kissing his feet in delight. The next morning, both father and son are discovered asleep in their seats at the breakfast table.

I have had insomnia for decades, waking in the night amid physical discomfort, troubling dreams, unexpected noises, or nothing at all. There is no alerting cry and no driving in circles looking at the moon. There is certainly no kissing of feet.

When my parents experimented with not rushing to the room where their daughter had begun to cry in the night, they discovered that I soon put myself back to sleep peacefully and without assistance. How did I do that? The unknown strategies of babyhood do not persist in adult life.

Recently, I watched a rerun of a TV show in which a woman demonstrates how to put her friend's crying baby to sleep with a recorded lullaby on an iPhone. I wouldn't have wanted the sounds of my mother's beautiful, familiar voice replaced by a preprogrammed lullaby, though I sometimes wish now that I had her musical voice to listen to when I wake with no language but a cry in the night.

---

113. Alfred Lord Tennyson, "In Memoriam," in *The Norton Anthology of English Literature*, vol. E, ed. Stephen Greenblatt et al., 9th ed.(New York: Norton, 2012) section 54, ll. 17-20, p. 1206.

WE SPEAK

"**Speak: intr. 1.** To utter words or articulate sounds with ordinary speech modulations; talk. **2a.** To convey thoughts, opinions, or emotions orally. **b.** *To express oneself.* **c.** To be on speaking terms. **3.** To deliver an address or a lecture. **4a.**To make a statement in writing. **b.** To act as spokesperson. **5a.** *To convey a message by nonverbal means.* **b.** *To be expressive.* **c.** To be appealing. **6.** To make a reservation or request. Often used with "for." **7a.** *To produce a characteristic sound.* **b.** To give off a sound on firing. Used of guns or cannon. **8.** *To make communicative sounds.* **9.** *To give an indication or a suggestion.* **tr. 1.** To articulate in a speaking voice. **2.** To converse in or be able to converse in (a language). **3a.** *To express aloud*; tell. **b.** To express in writing. **4.** [Nautical] To hail and communicate with (another vessel) at sea. **5.** *To convey by nonverbal means [italics mine]."*[114]

Long before we are verbal communicators, we speak. A baby's first cry includes definitions 2b, 5a, 5b, 7a, 8, and 9 of "speak" as an intransitive verb, along with definitions 3a and 5 of "speak" as transitive. (One might even add the nautical meaning of hailing another vessel while in the "sea" of the amniotic sac, or just emerging from it.) From the very beginning, we introduce ourselves with sound, convey a message by nonverbal means, give an indication or suggestion of our presence.

The cry is a complicated voicing, as Marilyn May Vihman tells us:

> In cry, produced with open mouth, we find
> the respiratory timing characteristic of
> speech, with brief intake of breath
> followed by prolonged expiration. . ..
> Vocalic [marked by or consisting of vowels]
> elements also derive primarily from cry, the
> only oral sound production in the early weeks
> of life. Finally, prosodic elements such as
> variation in intensity and pitch, rhythmic
> patterning, and phrasing are all present in cry
> long before they enter into vocal play.[115]

---

114. *American Heritage Dictionary*, 1329. The word "language" has as its derivation the Latin word, *lingua*, meaning "tongue." Ibid., 793.
115. Vihman, 104.

We leave the womb with a cry, announcing our first breath of life. King Lear says, "When we are born, we cry that we are come/To this great stage of fools."[116] We initiate our complicated conversation with the world we enter with a wail.

---

116. Shakespeare, *King Lear*: 4.6.176-177 (Conflated Text).

BETRAYAL

Listening to NPR, I hear a man say he remembers being a one-year-old in diapers, enjoying the comforting sounds of two singers on the radio. Later, when he learned the actual meanings of the words he had heard, he felt betrayed.

Golinkoff and Hirsh-Pasek write that in the first year of life, "the child relies on attention to the cadences in the sound stream to make sense of speech. After a bad night when the baby was up every hour teething, we could have said, `I hate you' in a loving tone to the baby and the baby could have been thrilled."[117] There was a Frenchman who thought "cellar door" was the most beautiful phrase in English.

I wonder if I ever felt "betrayed" after learning the meanings of word-sounds I had heard and loved. My first 200 words seem harmlessly sweet, this indoor and outdoor world of an eighteen-month-old baby. I could not have been betrayed by my new vocabulary, even words that would take on other connotations when I was older (for example, "pussy," "dirty"). The betrayal would have come from life itself, deepening and darkening the resonance of "no more," "that's all," "done," "doctor," "bye bye," and even "tummy" that would become the stomach where cancer came to take away the life of my father. Perhaps the only betrayal lies in the transience of what these so permanent words named: "daddy," "mama"—"no more."

How could I know then that a cheerful "bye bye," grown into "goodbye," could become an acknowledgment of irreversible leave-taking, parting forever? How could I know that "no more" playing or eating what I shouldn't have been eating in the first place or being read the same story multiple times could also come to mean no more of life itself? No, I don't think my sense of comfort in the word sounds I heard and repeated was ever betrayed. I'm glad I didn't know what I didn't know. Like the Frenchman's beloved "cellar door," the voicing was everything.

---

117. Golinkoff and Hirsh-Pasek, 200.

BODY PARTS

In Shakespeare's history play, *Henry V*, the French princess Katherin
is learning English words taught to her by an old gentlewoman named
Alice. Katherine says that it is necessary to learn to speak ("il faut que
j'apprenne à parler") in preparation for meeting her future husband, th
English King Henry V. The language lesson consists almost entirely of
names of various body parts. When the princess repeats the first two
words she hears ("de hand," "de fingres"), she immediately praises hers
as a quick learner and a good student and is complimented by Alice eve
though she never achieves the correct pronunciation of her new words:
hand, fingers, (finger)nails, arms, elbow, neck, chin, and foot. When
Katherine eventually asks for the name of an article of clothing ("la
robe"), Alice mangles the English word for gown ("le count"), producin
horrified reaction in the princess: "Ils sont les mots de son mauvais,
corruptible, gros et impudique" (these are bad, easily misconstrued,
vulgar, indecent words).[118]

The very first English words I heard would have been pristine, newly
born, without associations outside the context of a small parent-child
interaction. They would have been repeated and perhaps celebrated,
waiting for future retrieval or promptly forgotten. They would have bee
sheer sounds like those I heard in utero. They would have been home.

Our parents gave me and my brother many such lessons. Babies, lik
Katherine learning a new language for the first time, produce consisten
mispronunciations. The first words I learned would have been nouns:
specific, concrete, useful. Eleven of my recorded vocabulary words refe
to body parts: eye, hair, hand, knee, lap, mouth, nose, teeth, toes,
tongue, tummy. Over half of these nouns identify parts of the body mo
clearly visible in an intimate parent-child "conversation" and also most
clearly connected with speech. An inquiring *hand* might have touched
mouth, *teeth*, and *tongue*, along with a protruding *nose* and perhaps
whatever *hair* there was in the vicinity. An open *eye* would have allowe
a view of the means of articulating sound. *Tummy* might have been
uttered at some point, along with *lap*, in response to a complaint or a
request. The *toes*—well, touching my toes as I did then would be a fea
recalled wistfully later.

Like Shakespeare's French princess, babies must prepare linguistical
for a new vocabulary. Katherine's learning nouns for movable body pa
led her into her future. Learning the names for eye, mouth, and hand
would lead me to my own future life of teaching and writing.

---

118. Shakespeare, *Henry V*: 3.4.4-5, 15-16, 47-48.

WORDS I NEVER HEARD BEFORE

On the first day of a college course in written expression, I ask my students to write down five to eight words or phrases they like, either because of their meanings or because of their sounds. I add that they may include words in foreign languages or words they have invented. One student writes: "I enjoyed researching different words I had never heard before." Among the words on her list are "salubrious" and "pulchritudinous" but also "hygge" (Danish) and "querencia" (Spanish)—two languages I don't know. Hygge, Sarina tells me later, refers to a cozy feeling that comes from simple things, and querencia, she says, has to do with bullfighting, when a bull gathers up his energy.

Another student who knows a language I do know informs me that he likes the Latin word "quamquam" because it's fun to say. He also likes Xerxes, the name of the Persian king who organized the largest army the world had ever seen to invade Greece, for the same reason. My Shakespeare students take pleasure in repeating words that I use and they are hearing for the first time: liminal, microcosm, primogeniture. I take pleasure hearing the words my first-year students love. One offers me the word "duppy" which I am told, when I inquire, is Jamaican patois and means ghost. Another offers "redonkulous," without further comment—a word that seems midway between ridiculous and redundant.

Like my baby babble, my students' word lists could be the beginning of a writing life, even though they don't know that yet.

SCENES FROM SHAKESPEARE

My students perform scenes from Shakespeare's *Hamlet* for extra credit. They collect light-sabers for swords and use a large projection screen for an arras (a wall hanging or tapestry) to hide Claudius and Polonius. In the famous "To be, or not to be" scene, when Ophelia tells Hamlet that she has "remembrances of [his]/That I have longed long to redeliver," she hands Hamlet a banana. Halfway through the scene, the student playing Hamlet absentmindedly eats the banana. I was the only one in the room who laughed.

Ophelia later describes these "remembrances" as "Rich gifts."[119] "Banana" is the only three-syllable word in the list of my early vocabulary. Words of three syllables are relatively rare for one-to-two-year-old children.[120] Maybe I managed that singular verbal feat because a banana was a rich gift. Maybe I too ate the word I loved. Maybe I shouldn't have laughed.

* * *

The following week, my students perform another scene in which Hamlet harshly criticizes his mother, Gertrude, while Ophelia's father, Polonius, hides behind an arras, again represented by the large projection screen. The director, who is also playing Hamlet, has also placed the Ghost of Hamlet's father behind the arras to remain hidden from the audience's view. After Hamlet frightens his mother with his vehemence, she cries out for help. Polonius responds from his hiding place and Hamlet stabs him through the arras.

In the class performance, the student-director playing Hamlet, forgetting that she had positioned two actors behind the arras, mistakenly jabs the Ghost and then stabs Polonius with the copy of the play she is holding as she reads her lines. Polonius is slain by the text.

In Shakespeare's play, Polonius makes a habit of eavesdropping on other characters' conversations. This role is finally fatal.

Like every infant, I was an eavesdropper, even before my birth. Unlike the fate of Polonius, my eavesdropping eventually leads to continued listening: listening to the language my parents offered my future life long after they left.

---

119. Shakespeare, *Hamlet: 3.1.95-96, 103.*
120. Vihman, 201.

CONVERSATION

In my copy of Andrew Marvell's "To His Coy Mistress," I see I have written the word "conversation."

I ask students in my literature classes to join me in reading aloud the poems we study. I begin and they continue, observing caesuras (pauses dictated by rhythm or punctuation in a verse line), as I've taught them to do. What I have not taught them is the pronunciation of the unexpected or unknown words they may encounter as we merge our many voices into one continuous reading voice. If they hesitate, or ask for help, I may quietly pronounce words that have stumped them, like those names in Shakespeare's history plays that don't have as many syllables as they would think (Gloucester) or that change the expected sound of a vowel (Bolingbroke).

In the first stanza of Marvell's "To His Coy Mistress," the speaker tells his mistress that if they had many centuries in which to delay before sleeping together, he would wait:

> I would
> Love you ten years before the flood,
> And you should, if you please, refuse
> Till the conversion of the Jews.[121]

The student to whom these lines fell gamely took them on, and said,

> And you should, if you please, refuse
> Till the *conversation* of the Jews.

We continued our reading aloud, without comment on her misreading or its somewhat comic and mysterious implications.

I am one of the few Jewish professors at my Catholic college. Many of my students come from Catholic families, though their religious faith is not always that of their upbringing. Later in our discussion of the poem, I reread those lines and explained the reference to *conversion*. It occurred to me later that "the conversion of the Jews" was no more inexplicable than much else in the literature of earlier centuries and that it might be comforting to come across a word you could actually use in your daily life or in a classroom. And then I hoped that my students were being converted by their Jewish professor into joining a "conversation" with a very old poem.

---

121. Andrew Marvell, "To His Coy Mistress," in *The Norton Anthology of English Literature*, vol. B, ed. Stephen Greenblatt et al., 9th ed. (New York: Norton, 2012), ll. 7-10, p. 1797.

"AHPLANE"

Tucked inside my parents' copy of *The Child's Development and Health Record,* I find two undated poems in my own hand. The first is written on the back of a Christmas card: "In the merry month of May,/a peddler came this way./He said to me `how are you'/and I said to him `much better than you.'" A second attempt at rhyme is titled "My Monkey": "I had a little monkey and his name was cheep,/and he went for a ride in a big red jeep,/ when he got back he was all taters and torn,/and then I wish I had never been born."

I pass on.

At page 26, there is a report of "development" in my eleventh month:

> Stops to listen to plane. Says "ahplane."
> Makes noise of engine at question, "How
> does the airplane go?" Says "kitty" &
> "Tick Tock." Walks when being held by
> hand—Pushes stroller walking.

I recheck the list of my first 200 words. There is no "ahplane." I know that "ahplane" is only an approximation of the word it was after, but then so are "ta ta" and "ti ti." Perhaps "ahplane" was only uttered once, but we lived a few miles away from Washington National Airport (now Ronald Reagan National Airport) and I would have heard more than one "ahplane." Its absence on the list is a puzzling, perhaps inadvertent, omission.

What I hear in this tiny scene of the-word-that-failed-to-make-the-list is a dialogue. "How does the airplane go?," I am asked, and I respond with sheer sound, unrecorded in the list, like the unrecorded circumstances of its creation.

EITHER WAY, I'LL TAKE IT

A new mother reports on her 15-month-old son, Max, who calls her "Dada." "Every time I say, `Say Mama,' he goes, `Dada.' I can't quite tell if he thinks it's funny or if he's trying to be hurtful or if he simply thinks I am Dada. Either way, I'll take it."[122]

I wonder if my parents "took it" or if they worked hard to correct failures in language acquisition after the babbling stage. Then I remember the mother who proofread the manuscript of my first book, earning astonished praise from my editor; corrected the spelling of her son's grocery list; kept meticulous records of the times at which medications were to be administered to her husband as he lay dying in their Virginia home. I remember the father who carefully reviewed the writing of other lawyers at the Securities and Exchange Commission in Washington, D.C.; revisited all my college grades and received an embarrassed acknowledgment from Duke University that I had not been awarded appropriate honors at graduation; compiled a detailed report of his diagnosis of stomach cancer for two brothers and a sister in New York.

I don't think these were parents who took it either way.

---

122. "Carey Wilson," *People*, August 29, 2016, 68.

JUST BEING ABLE TO TALK

J. R. Martinez, after suffering burns over more than 40 percent of his body while serving as an infantryman (a word that shares its Latin derivative with "infant") during the Iraq war, became a first-time father in the spring of 2012. Martinez says of one-month-old Lauryn Anabelle (Belle): "I'm really looking forward to just being able to. . .talk with her—to hear what she'll say to me."[123] Parents' desire to talk to their baby is at times overwhelming, but so, at least at first, is the desire to hear what the child will say.

When baby Belle first begins to "talk," to whom is she actually speaking? Is it the parent who is talking "with her" or is her first speaking more private, to and for herself alone? These two kinds of speaking are often indistinguishable because one blends so easily into the other.

A baby's just being able to talk is trickier than it seems.

---

123. Monica Rizzo, "She's My Little Angel," *People*, June 18, 2012, 122.

THE CHILD'S DEVELOPMENT AND HEALTH RECORD

BY

HAROLD O. RUH, A.B., M.D.

CHIEF OF THE PEDIATRIC SERVICE OF ST. LUKE'S HOSPITAL, CLEVELAND, OHIO

AND

JUSTIN A. GARVIN, B.S., M.D.

VISITING PEDIATRICIAN OF ST. LUKE'S HOSPITAL, CLEVELAND, OHIO

D. APPLETON AND COMPANY

NEW YORK : : 1928 : : LONDON

FOREWORD

Periodic physical examinations enable the physician to detect abnormalities in the growth and development of children during the stage when they are most easily corrected. Parents should have full information concerning each examination in order to coöperate intelligently in maintaining the health of their children and in correcting their defects. A complete record of the child's past physical condition is frequently not available to the parents or to the physician at the time when it is most needed. The purpose of this book is to make such a record accessible.

Provision has been made for the recording in orderly sequence from birth through the age of fourteen years of those events and observations which have a direct bearing on the child's health and growth. When change of residence, consultation with a specialist, or other factors bring the child under the care of a different physician, the value of a résumé of his past history is evident. When the care of the child falls on individuals other than the parents, this book will supply them with a continuous account of the child's previous health.

Some of the recorded data, such as the dates of contagious diseases or of immunization against diphtheria and smallpox, are requested when a child enters school, goes to summer camp or enters college. Definite information of this kind is also of value during epidemics. In addition, the book will furnish in convenient form the data needed to establish birth status for passport purposes, or the information necessary for a marriage license or life insurance application. It may also be a valuable source of information in adult life in connection with a serious but obscure ailment.

It may be, too, that the child's health story will in later years have a certain sentimental value for him, for his parents, and for future generations.

HAROLD O. RUH
JUSTIN A. GARVIN

Cleveland

MY OWN LISTS

In my search for the first word I ever uttered, I learn many things that could interest no one but me. I weighed 6 pounds, 2 ounces at birth, and was 18 inches long. There is a handwritten record of my weight, taken twice a week, on Wednesdays and Sundays, and then every Sunday until I weighed 21 pounds, 12 ounces. At eighteen months, my length, recorded in the same hand, is 33 inches.

On a sheet of white lined paper, folded in half, is the note: "June 16—Baby cries a tear—12 days old." On June 28 (my wedding anniversary), the baby "laughed aloud in bath." Apparently, my development is being compared with benchmarks that other parents would have consulted in order to check on their own infants' progress. *The Child's Development and Health Record* states:

> Normal children vary widely in the rapidity of their development. The following list, which gives the approximate age at which the average child does certain things, will suggest to the mother some of the observations she should make, recording them in the book at the age when they occur.[124]

I make my own lists, comparing what would have been the expected development of babies with my own. The list on the left is taken from the first three pages of *The Child's Development and Health Record*. The list on the right reproduces my mother's comments on subsequent pages.

FIRST MONTH	SUSAN
Closes eyes in bright light	"Closes eyes in bright light." (second week)
Turns head toward light	"Turns to light." (second month)
Notices sound	"Starts at loud sounds." (second week)

---

124. Harold O. Ruh and Justin A. Garvin, *The Child's Development and Health Record* (New York: D. Appleton and Company, 1928), 1.

SECOND MONTH	SUSAN
Smiles	"Smiles and `talks' in response." (second month)
Has tears when crying	"Tears when crying (12 days old)."

I am two months old. What am I "talking" about?

Marilyn May Vihman notes that the baby's "first comfort sounds, defined as sounds produced in pleasurable interaction with the mother. . .and typically observed in the context of mutual gaze accompanied by smiling, are brief low intensity grunts or breathy sounds (sighs), which represent a `regression in vocalization' relative to the more varied phrasing and rhythms that have already developed in cry."[125] I try to imagine my grunting and sighing. It is harder to imagine that at this young age I could already be "regressing"!

THIRD AND FOURTH MONTH	SUSAN
Notices own hands	"Notices own hands." (third month)
Makes "cooing" sounds	"Given rattle, holds it and coos at it." (second month)
Fixes eyes on objects	[See previous two entries.]
Holds head erect	"Holds head erect, while held over shoulder for long periods at time." (second month)
Turns over	"Before 2 mos. old, turned over in crib from front to back."
Recognizes direction of sound	"Recognizes direction of sound." (third month) "Hearing very acute." (fourth month)

---

125. Vihman, 106.

Now I am "talking" to my rattle, the other noise-making entity close by, perhaps imitating its sounds, or perhaps waiting for it to respond to my own.

At the time of this writing, my mother had been dead for 28 years, the same number of years she lived before she gave birth to me. I wonder how it changed *her* relation to language to be newly in the presence of a non-speaking child to whom she wanted, needed, to speak, to give words of love, comfort, wonder.

Did she make up words, offer sounds that pleased her or made me smile? Did she imagine conversations we would grow into? Did she imagine a whole new speaking life for me, for us, even as I could say nothing?

Did she imagine that I would ever have to figure out a language with which to respond to a non-speaking mother?

FIFTH MONTH	SUSAN
Grasps playthings	"Plays with strings of beads, rattles." (third month)
Turns to watch moving objects	"Follows moving objects." (third month)
Makes sounds such as "Mum," "Da"	"Jabbering continuously."

A baby's invented words have been given various labels: "protowords," "quasiwords," "sensorimotor morphemes," and "phonetically consistent forms."[126] I seemed to enjoy making sounds with rattles, strings of beads, and my own protowords. Apparently, my continuous "jabbering" did not include references to "Mum" or "Da." This may have disappointed Mum and Da, but I was busy with my own invented language.

I wish I had some of it back now.

---

126. Hoff, 146

SIXTH MONTH	SUSAN
Laughs	"Laughs boisterously." (fourth month)
Recognizes persons other than mother or nurse	"Is conscious of strangers." (fifth month)
Tries to sit upright	"Tries to sit up when being held at feeding. Sits up with straight back when pulled up." (third month) "Tries to sit upright." (fifth month)

SEVENTH MONTH	SUSAN
Grasps and plays with toys	"Reaches for toys anywhere in play pen." (fifth month)
Realizes different or strange places	"First airing 43 weeks."
Supports weight of body on legs	"In crib and play pen, pulls self up and stands." (seventh month)
Sits well with support	"Sits alone for a few minutes." (fifth month)
Is conscious of strangers	"Is conscious of strangers." (fifth month)

EIGHTH MONTH	SUSAN
Sits alone	"Sits alone without support." (sixth month)
Stands with support	"In crib and play pen, pulls self up and stands." (seventh month)

NINTH MONTH	SUSAN
Holds out hands when picked up	"Holds out arms to be picked up." (ninth month)

In these months what seems of interest is my physical

prowess, such as it was: sitting upright alone and standing; reaching for toys; holding out arms to be lifted up higher. These movements seem so basic, so elemental. Many other mammals achieve them much more quickly. At a farm near Charlottesville, Virginia, I saw a horse give birth to a foal that immediately stood, shakily, beneath its mother's body.

Now I think of the other stage of life where we may again have difficulty sitting upright alone, standing, reaching for what is just beyond our grasp, needing to be lifted by stronger arms to a greater height than we can manage on our own.

TENTH MONTH	SUSAN
Stands alone	"Stands alone in play pen sometimes. Then, realizing it, she sits down quickly." (tenth month)
Says "Dada," "Mama"	"Says `Mama,' `Bye-Bye,' `Hi.'" (ninth month)

Is one of these my first word? I know that "Mama" often follows "Dada" in a baby's early vocabulary. Did I reverse that?

TWELFTH MONTH	SUSAN
Attempts to walk	"Walks around pen holding on with one hand. Very sure of self." (eighth month) "Walks when being held by hand." (eleventh month)
Indicates likes and dislikes	"Loves bath but dislikes cool water sponging." (second month) "Beginning to enjoy people's attentions." (eighth month) "Enjoys orange slice & toast. . . . Doesn't enjoy milk from glass—prefers bottle." (ninth month)

	"Great interest in strangers." (tenth month) "'Loves' her bunny and teddy bear." (eleventh month)

Have I learned the crucial word, *love,* in my eleventh month? The quotation marks stop me. I recheck the list of *l* words: "love" is clearly not there. And yet the feeling has preceded the word.

What comes next is a summary of achievements: toe-grabbing, drinking from a glass, waving in greeting or farewell, attempts at putting on shoes and pushing my own mode of locomotion, the inevitable toilet training, responding to certain commands ("Hold still," "Touch Mommy's Nose"). Then there is a frustratingly ambiguous note: "Understands many things." How this was ascertained I do not know. I gladly accept the truth of this assertion.

ONE YEAR	SUSAN
Attempts walking alone	"Walks at twelve months."
Uses one hand in reaching and can wave	"Reaches for toys anywhere in play pen. Grabs toes." (fifth month) "Waves bye-bye and hello." (ninth month)
Holds cup to drink from	"Begins to drink from glass." (sixth month)
Imitates simple acts	"Smiles and 'talks' in response." (second month) "Smiles in response to smiles." (third month) "Pats hands for "'patty cake.'" (seventh month) "Tries to put shoes on." (eleventh month) "Pushes stroller." (eleventh month)
and understands simple commands	"Responds to 'Hold still' and 'Put head down.'"

	Responds when put on seat for bladder and bowel training." (sixth month) "Ability to comprehend simple orders and actions now apparent. . . . Seems to understand `No-no' and `Come here,' etc." (ninth month) "Understands many things." (tenth month) "Understands orders to `Take Spoon,' `Touch Mommy's Nose,' `Hair,' `Brush Your Hair.'" (eleventh month)
Says "Dada," "Mama," and one or two other words	"Says `Mama,' `Bye-Bye,' `Hi.'" (ninth month) "Small vocabulary." (tenth month) "Says `ahplane.'" (eleventh month)

There is no list of my "small vocabulary" at ten months. My brother's vocabulary in his twelfth month is recorded: "mama, dada, see (fingers pointing), here, bow wow (deep tone), baby, Susan (Su Sa), down, up, out, shoe, hi there, bye bye, Trrrrr (for airplane)." With the exception of "see," "bow wow," and "Trrrrr," his small vocabulary could have been very like my own.

FIFTEEN MONTHS	SUSAN
Walks alone	"Walks at twelve months."

EIGHTEEN MONTHS	SUSAN
Uses five or more words	"Vocabulary counted up to 200, then stopped taking count. Combining 2 or 3 words." (eighteen months)

At approximately the age of one year, *The Child's Development and Health Record* suggests, the average child "understands simple commands." In my ninth month, my mother reports cautiously: "Ability to comprehend simple orders and actions now apparent. . ... Seems to understand `No-no' and `Come here,' etc. . ... Says `Mama,' `Bye-Bye,' `Hi.'"

Which of these, if any, was my first word?

Words, strictly defined, are "sequences of sounds that carry meaning."[127] Along with my mother's wary "seems," there is an "etc.," written in tiny letters, tucked in just after "Come here," suggesting that this list of understood words and phrases is incomplete. Was there an "etc." of lost, semi-intelligible "words" before more distinct versions could be identified?

When I pleased myself by "talking," in my second month of life, or jabbered continuously in my fifth month, was I, despite my mother's discretion in putting "talks" in quotation marks, speaking an invented first language, never to be recorded?

"For many children," Erika Hoff observes, "there is a transitional period between babbling and the appearance of the first word. During the transitional period, children produce their own invented words. These invented words are sound sequences children use with consistent meanings but that bear no discernible resemblance to the sound of any word in the target language."[128] My earliest language was that universal, incessant baby-babble: rapid flowing sound that *was* talk, self-directed, self-entertaining, and perhaps in some way intelligible, if it could be recovered and analyzed.

No doubt, none of us can confidently remember our first spoken word. How understandable that is, and how strangely disappointing. The search for a lost first utterance is a search for our lost originary language.

As Ingrid Bengis has said, "the real questions are the ones that intrude upon your consciousness whether you like it or not."[129]

---

127. Hoff, 170.
128. Ibid.
129. Ingrid Bengis, *Combat in the Erogenous Zone: Writings on Love, Hate, and Sex.* Quoted in "Chapter & Verse," *Harvard Magazine*, vol. 114, no. 6 (July-August 2010), 20.

BACKWARD/FORWARD

I turn toward light streaming in the window as I write, closing my eyes against the bright summer sun.

It is July. I hold my head erect as I look around; I smile and talk in response to others, visible and invisible. I start at loud sounds. Long before August I have noticed my own hands, followed moving objects, and recognized the direction of the many sounds floating through the open window—the steady drone of the mower on the front lawn, children's laughter in the courtyard, workmen replacing broken bricks in the back of our early-twentieth-century apartment building, robins and mockingbirds and mourning doves calling to one another, people chatting on cell phones as they pass by on the sidewalk, piano music escaping from a neighbor's window, a parent calling to a child to come indoors, giggles and squeals of two tiny girls in bathing suits darting through the spray of sprinklers on the grass, a lone dog barking somewhere. My hearing is still "acute," as recorded in my fourth month, and I wonder if during the summer days of my babyhood I was as overwhelmed by sounds as I am now.

I smell the cut grass and the fading of the giant linden tree's glorious scent. The mowing has moved to the backyard and is now incessant. There is a slight breeze and I begin to daydream. I go backward in time, before my birth. My gynecologist, Dr. Ann Strong, tells me that babies in the womb are "very responsive to sound, music, voices."[130] Suddenly I remember that my mother was singing when she was in labor, lying on rubber sheets before giving birth to me on a hot day in early June.

Erika Hoff affirms that "the auditory system is functioning in the fetus even before birth. The fetus will move in utero in response to external sound." Experimentation with fetuses and new-born babies "makes it clear that babies hear speech before birth and that they remember something about what they hear. . .. newborns show evidence of familiarity with the particular language their mothers spoke while the infants were in utero. . .. [B]abies hear and remember the prosodic contour of the speech their mothers produced."[131] I try to imagine the sounds I heard in that very different summer of 1940.

I listen again to the mower as if I had not looked out the window to identify the source of that unrelenting noise. It feels quite frightening. I close my eyes. It is more frightening. My eyes might be open in the

---

130. Dr. Ann Strong, interview, December 15, 2011.
131. Hoff, 148, 149, 162.

womb. "We don't officially know," Dr. Ann Strong says. "We don't think ambient light penetrates [the fetus in the womb]."[132]

I learn that a fetus' lungs don't mature until between 28 and 34 weeks; babies don't actually "breathe" (inhale oxygen) until they are born. "They inhale, swallow down, [amniotic] fluid; it goes through their intestines and they pee into the womb. . . .. The amniotic fluid is fetal pee."[133] The amniotic fluid is fetal pee! A circular intake and outflow of life-giving fluid: nothing is wasted.

Now I imagine my life before vision, breath, speech. I am a voiceless miracle of acute sensing of sounds, music and voices. How else could I spill forth into the regions of light except with a cry?

---

132. Dr. Ann Strong, interview, December 15, 2011.
133. Ibid.

Alice and Alfred Letzler

JUST TO HAVE ASKED

I have searched the records kept by those who can no longer speak to me for the first word I spoke to them. Now I wonder what these accounts of their child's development tell me about those who kept them, those who can only speak to me now through writing.

How simple it would have been just to have asked my parents, when I could finally form such a sentence, what word it was I first uttered in their presence. It is, of course, their *being present* that made possible the lists and notes that disclose their lives as well as mine. I can't return to my early life without the help of their attentive presence, but it is exactly that help that I have failed to see as footprints of lives not my own.

The record of a baby's health and development is a record of parents' noticing—*their* acute hearing; *their* recognizing the direction of the slightest sounds; *their* sensitivity to a great variety and range of sounds; *their* smiles; *their* following moving objects; *their* holding heads erect for long periods of time with an infant pressed against a shoulder; *their* entertaining themselves with talking to a baby not acclimated to language; *their* calling themselves "Mama" and "Daddy," losing their own names in the process even as they taught me mine; their joie de vivre recorded as my own.

DECODING

Inside *The Child's Development and Health Record* (beneath my unprepossessing crayon drawing of a brown house with six oddly shaped windows and a blue door), I find an undated 5" x 8" sheet of white unlined paper containing my parents' penciled handwriting. My mother begins: "Shows extreme ingenuity & inventiveness in building with blocks & play with Tinker Toy [sic]." Beneath is my father's telegraphic comment: "Extensive vocab.—shades of meaning—," and then a mysterious and uncharacteristically incomplete note: "[illegible] sentences the."

In my mother's hand follow two more entries:

> Recognizes colors.
> Knows alphabet and counts to ten.

Directly beneath her comments appears, once again, my father's smaller, hard-to-read handwriting:

> Remembers people's names—& characters in stories.

My mother continues:

> Rides tricycle.
> Interest in comics. Enacts all stories told her.
> Makes up stories of rather involved detail.
> Related a "dream" of fish in her bed.

I am noticing my parents noticing me.

They both have full-time Government jobs, commuting from Northern Virginia daily to Washington, D.C.[134] My mother spends time watching a child play with blocks and Tinker Toys long enough to infer (or imagine) "extreme ingenuity & inventiveness." My father listens not

---

134. My mother, Alice Parson Letzler, who had been a fourth-grade teacher in Roosevelt, Long Island, came to Washington, D.C., to take a position at the Civil Service Commission and was transferred to the Social Security Board where she continued working full-time until I was almost three years old. My father, Alfred Letzler, came to Washington from New York to take a position as an attorney with the Farm Credit Administration and then with the Office of Price Administration. He later became Assistant Director of the Office of Opinion and Review at the Securities and Exchange Commission.

Shows extreme ingenuity + inventiveness
in building with blocks + play with
Tinker Toy

Extensive vocab - shades of meaning -
involved sentences etc.

Recognizes colors

Knows alphabet and counts to ten
Remembers people's names - + characters in stories

Rides Tricycle

Interest in comics. Enacts all stories
Makes up stories of rather involved told her
Related a "dream" of fish in her bed

Catches + throws ball - "nuts"
Distinguishes between him - her - small +
Asks to go to toilet - often goes herself.
"Disease germs" - thumb sucking
Begins handle knife (+ forks previously)
Continents - countries - French
Telephone conversations.
Plays doctor, conductor, engineer, soldier,
etc.
Recognizes many animals - dog cat horse cow
lion camel zebra monkey bear giraffe leopard
rabbit duck chicken wolf panda tiger
moon stars sun clouds sunset

only to a child's store of words but to differing shades of meaning—and then he notices something else, lost to me now.

I look again at my father's illegible word. With a magnifying glass, I think I see an initial "i" followed by "n" and "u" and "sl," then "ue," ending with a "d" or an "l": INUSLUED/L. It makes no sense. Even the "the" seems a bit ghostly. Was my father rushing to enter his perceptions in between my mother's elegant handwriting? There is ample space waiting for his comment. Did they write side by side? Did my mother begin, then leave the rest of the page blank, and return later to continue her record? No, she never would have left my father's comment unfinished, had she seen it.

My mother's notes fill the top half of the page. My father inserts his notes after hers and then fills the bottom half of the page with his own record of his daughter's activities. He would have read her comments, but she may not have read his, for it would have been nearly impossible for my mother not to proofread any writing placed before her eyes, as her children well knew. Perhaps, because my father's profession involved nearly continuous writing, and he wrote well, she would not think to correct or complete any notation he made.

I wonder if my eyes are the first to study this small piece of paper with such intense concentration. They, after all, had their child before them, still developing. I, on the other hand, have before me neither the child nor her parents, just one more list with a mysterious "word": INUSLUED/L. I instinctively put quotation marks around "word." It seems only right that I experience the same difficulty identifying an unrecognizable word as did my parents listening to their baby "talk." I am now in the parental role of decoder, as if my father inadvertently left this sign of his own experience in transcribing and making legible the words of a child embarking upon language.[135]

In this tiny record of parental acts of noticing, my mother comments on the recognition of colors, alphabet, and numbers (up to ten). My father notes the remembering of names of people and also characters in stories. My mother records both performance ("Enacts all stories told her") and creation of stories ("Makes up stories of rather involved detail").

I do not remember any of this, but I see my father's concern with accuracy of memory and my mother's enduring interest in theatrical

---

135. Kyleelise Holmes Thomas suggests, "I wonder whether your father had written `involved.'" Email, August 4, 2013. Looking again at the "illegible" word, I think she may be right about my father's writing "involved sentences," then adding "the" as if intending to continue his observation.

performance, begun in her youth. My mother's comment on "the rather involved detail" of the stories her daughter told suggests her characteristic patience as a willing listener.

I gaze at the last entry in my mother's hand: "Related a `dream' of fish in her bed." Of course, I do not remember this dream, nor do I recall any similar dream at any point in my life. My mother's account is uninflected: no exclamation marks, no underlining—just quotation marks around "dream" like those that problematize my early "talking." Like the mysterious "inuslued/l," this dream is indeterminate. Did I dream about fish (singular or plural?) in my bed or did I dream in my bed about fish? What kind of fish was it: big, small, friendly, fierce, hungry with open jaws, quietly sleeping alongside me with my bunny and bear? Or was this one of my not-so-detailed made-up stories presented as a dream? Was it a daydream? Did I know the difference?

As for my mother's view, it seems that if I said it was a dream, it was a dream she listened to. I never would have heard (or, until now, seen) her quotation marks. There was an exchange, a confiding, between us, a telling that is only partly told in the writing, a small secret sharing that must have been established long before I understood its value and importance in my life.

How much is lost—and offered—in these telegraphic writings.

The bottom half of the page, in my father's handwriting, contains an independent list and his own quotation marks:

> Catches & throws ball; "bats."
> Distinguishes between him—her—small & big.
> Asks to go to toilet—often goes herself.
> "Disease germs"—thumb sucking.
> [Illegible] handle knife (& fork previously).
> Continents—countries—French.
> Telephone conversations. Plays doctor, conductor, engineer, soldier, nurse, etc. [There is the tantalizing "etc."]
> Recognizes many animals—dog cat horse cow lion camel zebra monkey bear giraffe buffalo rabbit duck chicken wolf panda tiger moon stars sun clouds sunset
> [He must be writing this quickly—without punctuation or a new heading for the final list.]

Years ago I published an experimental memoir about my mother,[136] but I never attended so closely to my father's life. How much more he must have known about me than I ever knew about him.

I noticed my mother's noticing me, even imagined it when it didn't really happen. I remember arriving home late from dates during high school and walking through the open door of my parents' bedroom. My whispered, "I'm home, Mom," would be followed by a sleepy, "That's nice, darling." Only much later did I learn that it was my father who lay awake, waiting for the porch light to go out, the front door to click shut and lock, and the ascending footsteps of his daughter as I quietly climbed the stairs to address my mother while he remained silent, finally able to join her in sleep.

My search for what is lost to me from my early childhood, my earliest utterance, becomes a discovery of much else that was lost.

---

136. Susan Letzler Cole, *Missing Alice: In Search of a Mother's Voice* (Syracuse: Syracuse University Press, 2007).

BACKWARDS IN TIME

"It is with our faces that we face the world, from the moment of birth to the moment of death," Oliver Sacks says. "Our age and our sex are printed on our faces."[137]

Though very nearsighted, newborn babies can see faces close to their own, probably starting with the face of the mother. They can distinguish when a face is attending to them and when it is turned away. They notice objects, alive or inanimate, that are of particular interest to those who are looking at them. By nine months, a baby can track another person's gaze. Alexandra Horowitz elaborates:

> These behaviors reflect the infant's burgeoning understanding that people have attention, attention that can light on objects of interest: a bottle, a toy, or them. Between twelve and eighteen months, they begin to engage in bouts of *joint attention* with others: locking eyes, then looking to another object, then back to eye contact. This marks a breakthrough: to achieve full "jointness" the infant must on some level understand that not only are they both looking together, they are *attending* together. They are understanding that there is some invisible but real connection between other people and the objects that are in their line of gaze. Once they do this, all hell can break loose.

This kind of visual attentiveness does not necessarily last: "We outgrow the habit of looking. . . . The child wonders at our crying, monitors our smiles, looks where we look; with age we are all still able to do all this, but we fall out of the habit."[138]

---

137. Oliver Sacks, 82.
138. Alexandra Horowitz, *Inside of a Dog: What Dogs See, Smell, and Know* (New York: Scribner, 2009), 142-143, 162-163.

And so I go backwards in time to look at my father looking, "to engage in bouts of *joint attention*," however belated.

"Catches & throws ball; `bats.'" There he is, throwing a ball to his daughter, watching her catch and return it. Of course, there are quotation marks around "bats," like the ones around my "talking" and a "dream" of fish, but clearly there is a small bat or bat-like implement, and my father instructing or allowing me to attempt to hit a ball with it.

I remember my father's love of baseball and his teaching of the game to Ken who wore a child's gray baseball uniform in admiration of his daddy's playing for the Cards, a local baseball team. I remember both of them watching professional baseball on television together in the summers as I passed by, always on my way elsewhere. Only now in his handwritten note, do I imagine his early attempts to share his love of baseball with his young daughter, an activity that couldn't hold much fun for him (as suggested by the quotes around "bats"), but which was important enough to engage in and to record.

"Distinguishes between him—her—small & big." My father notices my recognition of gender along with size. (Not a tall man himself, was he more concerned with size than I had noticed?) I remember his telling me that in school he would sometimes inadvertently offend another student viewed at a distance by not offering an identifying greeting because of his nearsightedness, the very condition of the baby he first held in his arms. I imagine his unconscious wagering that his child would not repeat his experience, hoping that I could make distinctions (in a much more complicated world) that would help me identify persons without causing embarrassment or offense.

My father notes, without further detail: "Asks to go to toilet—often goes herself." This is not a subject I am particularly interested in pursuing, but toilet-training and its completion are mentioned on various pages of *The Child's Development and Health Record*. I do not know if my father participated in cleaning up after early non-toilet-trained incidents or in re-diapering. I imagine he did, though it is oddly embarrassing to think about this now. What I see is his tendency to focus on progress rather than failure.

My mother's comments in the *Development* book are slightly more detailed: "Eating, sleeping, toilet habits continue satisfactorily" (eight months); "Toilet training excellent" (ten months); "Bladder control at night more often than not" (eighteen months); "No more bed-wetting at all" (twenty-one months). This is a subject that has already exhausted my interest. My parents emphasize improvement and self-reliance— and that is enough for me.

CORRESPONDING MOMENTS

I try to date the undated page of parental notes by looking for corresponding moments in *The Child's Development and Health Record*. It is not easy. That book offers one page of record-keeping for each month of a baby's life up to the age of one year. After that, there are pages available for every three months up to the age of three; every six months up to the age of six; every twelve months up to the age of fourteen.

For the first three months, there is a blank page reserved for snapshots, with the slightly comic recommendation of "pictures with as little clothing as possible." After the sixth month, an otherwise blank page asks, "when possible," for "pictures showing facial expression and action"; after the twelfth month, "a picture in a standing position will show graphically his [sic] progress." At five years, "pictures of the child learning to walk, on kiddie-car, running, on tricycle, etc., will show steps in his development." A single snapshot page simply announces: "Six, Seven, Eight, Nine and Ten Years." At age fourteen, where the record-keeping is to end, there is a single-page note: "Eleven, Twelve, Thirteen, and Fourteen Years."[39]

There are no snapshots on any of the pages.

---

139. Ruh and Garvin, 17, 21, 28, 43, 50, 55.

SNAPSHOTS OF FIRST THREE MONTHS

(Pictures with as little clothing as possible are preferable.)

A correspondence between my parents' inked notes in the *Development* book and their penciled comments on toilet-training might suggest a description of a baby about twenty-one months old, but not necessarily. "Recognizes colors" might correspond to the inked note, "Knows colors," when I am two years and nine months, but my mother may have made a distinction between "knows" and "recognizes."

There is a similar problem in linking the penciled comment, "Telephone conversations," with my mother's inked note, "Rudimentary conversation carried on over phone," when I am two. An inked note in the *Development* book reports that my brother "counts to ten" at the age of two. In a penciled note, I "count to ten."

* * *

A piece of undated paper remains undated, resisting interpretation, like an unintelligible word, or an "etc.," or a pair of quotation marks.

* * *

I return one last time to my father's list, focusing on a phrase in quotes and another illegible word.

> "Disease germs" — thumb sucking.
> [Illegible] handle knife (& fork previously).

"Disease germs" sounds like the noun-jumbled phrase a child might utter. Is my father unconsciously mimicking that, just using shorthand or inscribing a term a pediatrician used? His terse report gives a description of an activity (his daughter is still sucking her thumb) and an implied reason for trying to prevent it. As a child, and as an adult, I was always aware of the rational judgment of my father without always noticing the attentiveness that preceded it.

My attention turns to the unintelligible word beneath the note on thumb sucking. With a magnifying glass and a little imagination, I can almost make out "Beginning," although the "B" looks like an "R." There is an "e" followed by a "g" or "j," an "i" and "n" (or possibly two), and a final "g" or "y": B/R E G/J IN [maybe another "N"] G/Y. Whatever handling of forks and then knives I mastered, I cannot master the language that reports its progress. I am a decoder who keeps trying and failing to decode.

The next penciled entry is fully legible and mysterious: "Continents—countries—[then in smaller, fainter handwriting] French." This notation is as bereft of detail as the next one: "Telephone conversations." Apparently my father is noticing, or trying to create, an interest in other continents and countries. I look again at the word, "French." Suddenly I recognize my mother's handwriting. It is her "F," not his. She has added this faded word to my father's notes. Is this a private joke? She knew French. Is she playfully telling my father that his daughter's babble suggests a language spoken in another country, another continent? What I know now is that she read his list, and that this undated page is a kind of dialogue, a collaboration, his comments intermingled with hers, hers with his.

"Plays doctor, conductor, engineer, soldier, nurse, etc." Except for nurse and doctor (my pediatrician was a woman), these professional roles my father observed me enacting were, at that time, mainly male (and did not include what I ultimately became: a college professor and a writer). Were these references to characters in books he and my mother read to me or characters pictured in books I was shown? I wonder if my father assumed I was playing a certain role by watching me or if he played with me until he learned whom I was impersonating. He may have identified my play-acting by speaking to me in an assumed role. Perhaps he took part, willingly or unwillingly, in my small performances. I will never know.

It is his "etc." that opens more doors than I can enter. He reports what he notices and he notices more than he reports. In his *et cetera* lies a world of unknowns.

The next-to-last list does not leave much to the imagination. "Recognizes many animals—dog cat horse cow lion camel zebra monkey bear giraffe buffalo rabbit duck chicken wolf panda tiger." Then my father adds, again without punctuation, as if still writing rapidly, "moon stars sun clouds sunset," with no introductory note.

The animals on my father's list could have been in picture-books or at the Washington zoo or stuffed and crowded into my bed with me. Perhaps my father shared my passion for animals. All I really know is that I didn't notice this in his life and he did notice it in mine.

The last entry is, from my adult perspective, quite romantic: "moon stars sun clouds sunset." These celestial bodies and events seem to be "recognized," but only "moon" is included in the list of my early vocabulary. What escapes the list is as tantalizing as what is on it.

* * *

There it is: an undated page, with recognitions rather than recorded language and with activities that cry out for more specificity: telephone conversations, stories enacted, building (what?) with blocks, knives and forks, colors and countries and continents, French, *et cetera*.

I gaze at my father's last list. Moon, stars, sun, clouds, and sunset may have appeared in books as well as in our shared experience. Oddly my father has not included the word "recognizes" in introducing the final group of words. This last list, with its lack of both punctuation and verb, seems rushed, like a child's stream of just-learned sounds.

My father has already noticed "shades of meaning" in my "extensive vocabulary." Now he suggests that I can notice different kinds of natural light as well: sun, stars, moon, sunset.

Ambient light may not penetrate the womb; the fetal eye may not see much more than shadows. I imagine my father watching me watch the setting sun. I imagine my parents watching the gradual fading of light, the descent into darkness.

I have come to the end of my impossible search.
I am done.

I close my eyes.
I open them to the light.
I cry out.
I hear my first utterance at last.

INEXPRESSIBLE

I tried in a previous book to express the inexpressible, the loss of what as a child I thought would go on forever: being together on this earth. I cannot say I am "unmothered" or "unfathered" by the deaths of my parents. They were always there during my life, and they are still here in these pages, but there is now a silence in this one-way stream of language that, so far as I can tell, was never characteristic of our lives. I write into that silence just as they once spoke into my own.

When I was an infant, there were experiences I could not put into words. Those would have been very simple things, all having to do with life itself. Ahead of me, of us, lay language in all its beckoning abundance, sufficient to the task at hand: decoding the world we inhabited together. What was inexpressible was temporary, a stage to be gotten through. Young parents with full-time jobs might have felt some ambivalence as their infant with her growing vocabulary began to ask many more questions and demand responses, probably a lot of them repetitions of previous responses. And yet they persisted in their loving care for the process of the inexpressible becoming expressible.

My parents gave me language even as I barely knew what to do with it. Now that I know what to do with it, I find myself once again in the presence of the inexpressible.

EPILOGUE

When I last saw my mother conscious, she, without at all wanting to fell asleep during the final hour of my visit home. I remember sitting by her side, looking at her sleeping face, while the woman Ken and I had just hired to stay in the house 24 hours a day peeked at me intermittently from the next room. I saw myself as she might have, wondering why I didn't leave, prepare for my journey back to New Haven, chat with her, read the newspaper, gaze through the full-length glass door at the roses blooming in the backyard. I saw myself watching my mother sleep, peacefully, just as, I realize, she must have done when I was an infant: present without boredom, without desire for distraction, without worrying about what else one could or should be doing or where else one could or might be. I was fully employed in this watching, not knowing then that it would be the last before her brief hospitalization, coma, and death five days later.

When she awakened, I was still there. As her eyes met mine, I saw a sudden pleasure-filled surprise. She may have thought that I had already left for my train without continuing the conversation that had paused while she napped. She may have thought that I would have been wandering restlessly around the house, always on the move, as I had been when she was my age and I was in my twenties. Maybe in her dreams she had been preparing to meet my arrival at Washington's Union Station, as she once was able to do, and was startled to see me sitting there by her side. Or maybe she was dreaming that we were on our last holiday together, in a horse-drawn buggy, looking at flowers and trees and birds she alone could identify while the brown horse pulling our carriage stepped delicately to the side of each rain-filled puddle on the path. But nothing in that earlier summer trip produced the smile I saw in her eyes when she saw me smiling, still there, still watching. We talked for a few minutes before I had to leave. I remember quoting lines from Wordsworth's Intimations of Immortality ode; we kissed and hugged goodbye. I never saw her eyes open that way again.

Now I reverse our roles in my mind. I imagine her patient watching, her loving gaze, as I nap. I imagine waking in the third month of my life, smiling "in response to smiles"; even in my second month, smiling and "'talk[ing]' in response"; in my eighth month, "much joie de vivre." I would not have expected my mother to be wandering, about to leave, elsewhere. I would bask in her gaze, return it, feel it to be enough. That mutual gaze would have been our first "conversation." My first dialogue outside the womb would have been conducted by the agency of sight. In the dark pre-birth world of shadows and outlines, sound would have been a one-way path of communication.

In the world of late summer light, in which I last saw my mother fully conscious, there was no need of speech. Her awakening eyes said everything that needed saying. And yet we spoke. That was what mother and daughter had learned to do together: listen, look, talk. At the end of her life we were recapitulating the beginning of mine.

During my final visit with my mother a few days later in a Northern Virginia hospital, there was no dialogue, only a one-way path of sound, this time coming from child to parent. My mother was now in the dark but not sound-proof world of my own earliest life. My words reached her ears but her language was not available to me. I no more knew her last unspoken words to me than I know my first unspoken words to her. In the coma of her final days, she must have "recognized [the] direction of sound," as she recorded in my third month of life; she may even have "recognized [the] direction of [the] slightest sounds," and, in her own way, responded with a "great variety and range of sounds," as she recorded in my fifth month.

I had no *Parent's Development and Health Record* in which to note such things as I observed or imagined. There was no thought of that at all. There was attention to shifts in position, signs of distress, need for support, taking in of nutrients, changes in heartbeat, breathing, signs of life—and there was talking, talking past the hour when the doctor pronounced my mother's death. We ended as we began, one of us talking to a speechless other, with no sense of why that wasn't exactly what we ought to be doing.

WORKS CITED

Angier, Natalie. "African Tribesmen Can Talk Birds Into Helping Them Find Honey." *New York Times,* July 24, 2016, 6N.
_____. "Profiles in Science/ Elizabeth S. Spelke: From the Minds of Babes." *New York Times,* May 1, 2012, D4.

"A Real Brain Wave: How to Give Voice to the Speechless." *The Economist,* vol. 430, no. 9140 (April 27, 2019), 70.

Bedell, Jillian Raucci. Email correspondence, April 17, 2018.

Bengis, Ingrid. *Combat in the Erogenous Zone: Writings on Love, Hate, and Sex.* Quoted in "Chapter & Verse," *Harvard Magazine,* vol. 114, no. 6 (July-August 2010), 20.

Berenbaum, May. "Understanding Apis." *Times Literary Supplement,* July 8, 2016, 23-24.

Boardman, Dr. Samantha. "ON *the* BRINK." In Edward Mapplethorpe, *One: Sons & Daughters.* Brooklyn: powerHouse Books, 2016.

Brzowsky, Sara. Email correspondence, July 5, 2018.

Carey, Benedict. "Hope for the Voiceless: Scientists Decode Brain's Vocal Signals." *New York Times,* April 5, 2019, B4. "Carey Wilson." *People,* August 29, 2016, 68.

Carroll, Lewis. *Alice in Wonderland: Authoritative Texts of Alice's Adventures in Wonderland, Through the Looking-Glass, The Hunting of the Snark.* Edited by Donald J. Gray. 2nd ed. New York: W.W. Norton & Company, 1992.

Cave, Damien. "American Children, Now Struggling to Adjust to Life in Mexico." *New York Times,* June 19, 2012, A3.

Cepelewicz, Jordana. "Your Brain on Physics." *Scientific American,* vol. 315, no. 2 (August 2016), 15.

Chang, Kenneth. "Up Close and Wearing Heat-Resistant Shades, Probe Spots `Campfires on the Sun.'" *New York Times,* January 17, 2020, A17.

Cole, Susan Letzler. *Missing Alice: In Search of a Mother's Voice.* Syracuse: Syracuse University Press, 2007.

"Computer Says: Oops." *The Economist,* vol. 420, no. 8998 (July 16, 2016), 65.

Corballis, Michael C. *From Hand to Mouth: The Origins of Language.* Princeton: Princeton University Press, 2002.

de Waal, Frans. *Are We Smart Enough to Know How Smart Animals Are?* New York: Norton, 2016.

Elliott, Elisa. *Eve.* New York: Bantam Books, 2010.

Epps, Wayne, Jr. "In a High-Tech Era, Ball Clubs Still Talk With Their Hands." *New York Times,* July 14, 2016, B9.

Firestone, Chaz and Brian J. Scholl. "Cognition does not affect perception: Evaluating the evidence for `top-down effects.'" http://perception.research.yale.edu/preprints/Firestone-Scholl-BBS.pdf. Accessed July 12, 2016.

Gholipour, Bahar. "Can We Learn How to Forget?" *Scientific American,* vol. 315, no. 2 (August 2016), 17.

Goldberg, Natalie. *Old Friend from Far Away.* New York: Free Press, 2007.

Golinkoff, Roberta Michnick and Kathy Hirsh-Pasek. *How Babies Talk: The Magic and Mystery of Language in the First Three Years of Life.* New York: Penguin, 2000.

Goldman, Russell. "Korean Words, From an Elephant." *New York Times,* May 27, 2016, A6.

Gopnick, Adam. "Baby Face." In Edward Mapplethorpe, *One: Sons & Daughters.* Brooklyn: powerHouse Books, 2016.

_____. "Dog Story: How did the dog become our master?" *The New Yorker,* August 8, 2011, 30.

Gorman, James. "These Monkeys Make Tools, but Don't Use Them." *New York Times,* October 25, 2016, D2.

Greenblatt, Stephen. "The Answer Man." *The New Yorker,* August 8, 2011, 30.

Greene, Brian. *Until the End of Time: Mind, Matter, and Our Search for Meaning in an Evolving Universe.* New York: Alfred A. Knopf, 2020.

Gustke, Constance. "For Effective Brain Fitness, Do More Than Play Simple Games." *New York Times,* July 9, 2016, B5.

Haupt, Lyana Lynn. *Pilgrim on the Great Bird Continent: The Importance of Everything and Other Lessons from Darwin's Lost Notebooks.* New York: Little, Brown and Company, 2006.

Henry, Brian. "Elegy Elegy." *New York Times Magazine,* May 29, 2016, 17.

Hirsh-Pasek, Kathryn and Roberta M. Golinkoff. *Action Meets Word: How Children Learn Verbs.* Oxford: Oxford University Press, 2006. http://www.oxfordscholarhship.com/view/10.1093/acprof:oso/97801. Accessed January 30, 2013.

Hoff, Erika. *Language Development.* 4th ed. Belmont, CA: Wadsworth, Cengage Learning, 2009.

Horowitz, Alexandra. *Inside of a Dog: What Dogs See, Smell, and Know.* New York: Scribner, 2009.

_____. *On Looking: Eleven Walks with Expert Eyes.*
New York: Scribner, 2013.

Horowitz, Seth S. *The Universal Sense.* New York: Bloomsbury,
2012.

Hurford, James R. *The Origins of Grammar: Language in the Light
of Evolution.* Oxford: Oxford University Press, 2012.

Joyce, James. *Ulysses.* New York: Random House, 1946.

Kaku, Michio. *The Future of the Mind: The Scientific Quest to
Understand, Enhance, and Empower the Mind.* New York: Random
House, 2014.

Keating, Caitlin and Nicole Weisensee Egan. "Life Without Mom."
People, March 7, 2016, 56-57.

Kincaid, Jamaica. *See Now Then.* New York: Farrar, Straus and
Giroux, 2013.

Klass, Perri. "Writing to Learn." *New York Times*, July 21, 2016,
D6.

Klein, Joanna. "A Language's Origins in a Few Small Bites."
New York Times, March 19, 2019, D4.

_____. "Want to Identify Proteins? Just Listen."
New York Times, October 25, 2016, D2.

Letzler, Kenneth. Email correspondence, June 23, 2018.

Lewis, Charlton T. *A Latin Dictionary for Schools.* New York:
American Book Company, 1916.

Loy, James D. and Kent M. Loy. *Emma Darwin: A Victorian Life.*
Gainesville: University Press of Florida, 2010.

Lupyan, Gary. "The Centrality of Language in Human Cognition"
(2015), 4. http://sapir.psych.wisc.edu/papers/lupyan_CentralityOf
Language.pdf. Accessed July 11, 2016

Lupyan, Gary and Benjamin Bergen. "How Language Programs the
Mind." *Topics in Cognitive Science* (2015),5,2.
http://sapir.psych.wisc.edu/papers/lupyan_bergen_2015.pdf.
Accessed July 11, 2016.

Manjoo, Farhad. "Virtual Reality's Unsettling Rabbit Hole."
New York Times, June 23, 2016, B1.

Mapplethorpe, Edward. *One: Sons & Daughters.* Brooklyn:
powerHouse Books, 2016.

McEwan, Ian. *Nutshell.* New York: Doubleday, 2016.

Meyer, Julien. "The Whistled Sound." *Scientific American*, vol.
316, no. 2 (February 2017): 65, 64.

Montz, Dr. Lynn. Email correspondence, September 10 and 13, 2011.

Morell, Virginia. *Animal Wise: The Thoughts and Emotions of*

Our Fellow Creatures. New York: Crown, 2013.
Morrison, Toni. *The Source of Self-Regard: Selected Essays, Speeches, and Meditations*. New York: Alfred A. Knopf, 2019.
"Mothers who went to Hunter College really do know best." *New York Times*, May 12, 2019, N14-15.
Murphy, Kate. "Do You Believe in God, or Is That a Software Glitch?" *New York Times*, August 28, 2016, SR5.
Nuwer, Rachel. "Eggshell Education." *Scientific American*, vol. 314, no. 6 (June 2016), 20.
Oates, Joyce Carol. *The Lost Landscape: A Writer's Coming of Age*. New York: HarperCollins, 2015.
Pareles, Jon. "Chasing His Muse, at the Genetic Level." *New York Times*, January 22, 2017, AR14.
Peterson, Roger Tory. *A Field Guide to the Birds*, 2nd ed., rev. Boston: Houghton Mifflin, 1947.
Pinsky, Robert. "Window," *The Want Bone*. New York: Ecco Press, 1990.
Piston, Walter. *Orchestration*. New York: Norton, 1955.
Rizzo, Monica. "She's My Little Angel." *People*, June 18, 2012, 122.
Rosenberg, Monica. "Brain connections predict how well you can pay attention." *The Conversation* (2015). https://theconversation.com/brain-connections-predict-how-well-you-can-pay-attention-51082. Accessed July 9, 2016.
_____. Email correspondence, July 12, 2016.
Rosenblatt, Roger. *The Boy Detective: A New York Childhood* (New York: HarperCollins, 2013), 88.
_____. *Kayak Morning: Reflections on Love, Grief, and Small Boats* (New York: HarperCollins, 2012).
Rowland, Katherine. "We Are Multitudes" (2018), 8, 5. https://aeon.co/essays/microchimerism-how-pregnancy-changes-the-mothers-very-dna. Accessed June 18, 2018.
Ruh, Harold O. and Justin A. Garvin. *The Child's Development and Health Record*. New York: D. Appleton and Company, 1928.
Sacks, Oliver. *The Mind's Eye*. New York: Random House, 2010.
Sahn, Seung. Foreword, *Chanting with English Translations and Temple Rules*. Cumberland, R.I.: Kwan Um School of Zen, 1996, v-vi.
Schulz, Kathryn. "Losing Streak: Reflections on two seasons of loss." *The New Yorker*, February 13 & 20, 2017, 75.
Sengupta, Somini. "'Big Brother'? No, It's Parents." *New York Times*, June 26, 2012, B4.

_____. "Tools to Control a Child's Technology."
New York Times, June 26, 2012, B4.

Shakespeare, William. *The Norton Shakespeare, Based on the Oxford Edition.* Edited by Stephen Greenblatt et al. New York: Norton, 1997.

Siegel, Daniel J. *The Developing Mind: How Relationships and the Brain Interact To Shape Who We Are.* 2nd ed. New York: The Guilford Press, 2012.

Smith, Zadie. *Swing Time.* New York: Penguin Press, 2016.

Solomon, Andrew, "YOU WILL KNOW THEM *by* THE LIGHT IN THEIR EYES". In Edward Mapplethorpe, *One: Sons & Daughters.* Brooklyn: powerHouse Books, 2016.

Spelke, Dr. Elizabeth S. Quoted by Natalie Angier, "Profiles in Science/Elizabeth S. Spelke: From the Minds of Babes." *New York Times*, May 1, 2012, D4.

Stern, Daniel N. *Diary of a Baby.* New York: Basic Books, 1990.

Streitfeld, David. "Chasing Pokémon In Search Of Reality in a Game." *New York Times*, July 22, 2016, B1.

Strong, Dr. Ann. Interview, December 15, 2011.

Tattersall, Ian. "At the Birth of Language." *New York Review of Books*, vol. 53, no.13 (August 18, 2016), 28.

Tennyson, Alfred Lord. "In Memoriam." *The Norton Anthology of English Literature.* Vol. E, ed. Stephen Greenblatt et al., 9th ed. New York: Norton, 2012. Section 54, ll. 17-20, p. 1206.

Thomas, Kyleelise Holmes. Email correspondence, August 4, 2013; November 23, 2016; December 8, 2016.

Vihman, Marilyn May. *Phonological Development: The Origins of Language in the Child.* Cambridge: Blackwell, 1996.

Wade, Nicholas. "Meet Luca, Ancestor of All Living Things." *New York Times*, July 26, 2016, D1.

Welty, Eudora. *One Writer's Beginnings.* Cambridge: Harvard University Press, 1984.

Zimmer, Carl. "In Brain Map, Gears of Mind Get Rare Look." *New York Times*, July 21, 2016, A1, A17.

_____. "Monkeys Could Talk, But Their Brains Aren't Wired for It." *New York Times*, December 13, 2016, D2.